L. Olson 2/09

Also by Chris Crouch

Getting Organized: Improving Focus, Organization and Productivity

The Contented Achiever: How to Get What You Want and Love What You Get (with Don Hutson and George Lucas)

Simple Works: Simple Ideas to Make Life Better (with Susan Drake)

being productive

LEARNING TO GET MORE DONE WITH LESS EFFORT

Chris Crouch

Dawson
PUBLISHING

Dawson Publishing
3410 S. Tournament Drive
Memphis, TN 38125

Printed in the United States of America.

Cover design: Venue Advertising

For information on quantity discounts for bulk purchases, special sales or use in corporate training programs, please contact Dawson Publishing at 901.748.2142 or sales@dawsonpublishing.com.

ISBN-13: 978-0-9758680-5-8
ISBN-10: 0-9758680-5-5

2008938832

Is This Book for You?

There are two approaches to living a more productive life. You can attempt to squeeze more productivity out of a day with little or no concern for the price you might pay in terms of excessive stress, fatigue, burnout and compromising your overall mental and physical well-being. Or, you can focus on sound ideas and strategies that *offer solid productivity gains along with the potential to maintain a balanced life*. This book is for people who prefer the latter approach.

For the last decade or so I have focused on teaching people how to live more focused, organized and productive lives. Clients, life and career coaches, productivity trainers, interviewers, friends and others often ask me, "What issue or issues do you run into most often? What are the main productivity killers in the workplace today?" In this book I offer 24 answers to this question. There are many more productivity-killing issues in the workplace, but these are the issues I encounter most often.

The issues and ideas are somewhat randomly presented in this book. At times I felt a slight need to present certain ideas before others, since one might help lay the groundwork for better understanding another. You can either read the chapters in the order they are presented or scan the Contents page and explore the ideas on a stand-alone basis. You might also find that separate chapters offer slightly different approaches for addressing the same underlying problem. Pick the approach that you feel will work best for you based on your particular work style and work environment.

I'll keep listening to everyone and continue to share productivity ideas with you through my Web site (www.dmetraining.com), my blog (www.chriscrouch.typepad.com), future books and courses. I also encourage you to contact any of our Certified *GO System*© Trainers throughout the United States and Canada (www.gosysteminfo.com) and ask them for assistance. They are a great bunch of dedicated people who love helping others become more focused, organized and productive.

Here are a few additional comments to help you decide if this book is for you:

- This is a business book and is focused on improving productivity in the workplace. You can use many of the ideas in other areas of your life. However, this book will primarily focus on business applications.
- This book is for people who are willing to challenge some of their current assumptions about what it takes to live a productive life. No new behavior takes place unless you challenge and alter some of your current beliefs.
- This book is for people who desire to explore a variety of high-quality productivity ideas with a minimum investment of reading time.
- People pay attention when something is interesting and relevant to their situation. This book focuses on common issues you are likely to encounter in your workplace.
- I won't overpromise and claim that every idea in this book will work for everybody, in every situation. I do

promise to stay extremely practical and only offer ideas that I believe will work for most people, in most typical work situations.

- This book is written as if the ideas being presented are for your use. However, you can also use these ideas to help others in your role as a leader/manager, coach, mentor, teacher, consultant, etc.
- For many years, I have been involved with an informal learning group. A group of my friends and I meet monthly to explore topics and share ideas to help each other live more joyful and productive lives. I highly recommend that you form such a group. Each chapter of this book can serve as a topic for these monthly learning group meetings.
- Each chapter is short, covers one productivity idea and is presented in the following three-part format.

  What? (an explanation of the main idea)

  So What? (more information on the idea including why the idea is relevant in terms of improving productivity)

  Now What? (practical suggestions, when relevant, for following up on the idea or implementing and applying the idea)

In summary, simplicity, practicality and brevity govern the design of this book. Sydney Smith best captured the spirit of this book in his saying, "The writer does the most who gives the reader the most knowledge and take from him the least time." If the above elements appeal to you, I invite you to read this book.

Contents

1
Awareness: The Best First Step

What?

Awareness means knowing something exists because you notice it or realize it is happening. Awareness is something most of us take for granted. It is human nature to assume we are always aware of important things going on in our lives. However, this is not always the case, as you will see in the following two stories.

How can awareness affect your productivity as an employee? Imagine for a moment you work as a security guard at the entrance/exit gate of a large manufacturing facility. Your primary job is to prevent employee theft. Therefore, you are most productive when there is zero employee theft. A typical workday for most plant employees begins at 8:00 a.m. and ends at 5:00 p.m. Since the gate must be monitored 24 hours a day, you are part of a team of three guards who work in eight-hour shifts. The shifts are scheduled so that a change of guard will not occur when most employees are coming or going for the day. Therefore, you are assigned to guard the gate from 7:30 a.m. until 4:30 p.m.

Once a week, one particular employee comes up to the gate at about 4:20 p.m. with a wheelbarrow full of trash and worthless junk. He tells you, "My boss said for me to get rid of this crap before quitting time. I'm going to take it outside the gate and dump it in the woods." Not being a conscientious environmentalist (remember, I said use your imagination), you quickly glance at the contents of his wheelbarrow, recognize it as trash and worthless junk, realize it is about time for you to get off for the day and wave him through the gate. You don't want any hassle 10 minutes before quitting time. Soon afterwards, the guard working the next shift shows up and you leave for the day.

At the end of the year, company accountants perform an audit and are surprised to discover that during the year someone in the purchasing department ordered 52 Ames True Temper, heavy-duty, corrosion-proof, contractor wheelbarrows, with 10 cubic foot trays, 2-ply pneumatic tires and steel front tray braces, at a cost of $236.56 each. A total wheelbarrow expense of $12,301.12 for one year seems excessive to the in-charge accountant. When the puzzled accountant sends his young assistant to locate the wheelbarrows and find out why so many are being ordered, not one wheelbarrow can be found! No one knows where they are...until they ask you!

Once they discover what happened to the wheelbarrows, you are demoted. They take you off the front gate and make you walk around the huge manufacturing facility, more than 26 acres, monitoring employee theft. In addition to problems with people stealing things and taking them outside the company, it has come to management's attention that some employees are stealing materials from other departments to make their own department's bottom line look better and increase their incentive payouts.

One day you stumble upon a group of employees who appear to be doing just that. Suspicious looking employees from Department A have backed a truck up to a pile of materials belonging to Department B. You come around the corner and surprise the Department A employees who are standing near their truck, holding materials...caught red-handed. You say, "Hey, what are you guys doing?" One quick-thinking Department A employee says, "Our boss told us to dump all of this scrap material somewhere away from our department!" You reply, "No way! You can't just dump that stuff here. Load that stuff back on your truck, and take it back to your own department!" The rogue employees do not argue with you. They quickly comply with your orders and hurry off. You detect a faint smile on the quick-thinking employee's face. Luckily, you showed up just in time to stop these guys from taking advantage of another department...or did you?

So What?

So what is the moral of these two stories? You can't fix a problem, and sometimes you can't even see that you have a problem, without a certain level of awareness. I realize that the person in the story was easily tricked and that such a thing could probably never happen to you...or could it? For a moment, imagine the wheelbarrows and the pile of materials represent your time and energy (which is significantly more expensive than $236.56 per week). If you do not remain keenly aware of the productivity thieves that exist in the modern workplace, they will rob you of your time and energy in the same way the wheelbarrow thief and rogue employees perpetrated their crimes. You may think you are doing the right thing, but you are actually doing the opposite. For example, here are some of the things that frequently happen to otherwise very smart people in today's typical workplace. Are these things good for your productivity or not?

- Is working significantly more than eight hours a day a productivity enhancer or productivity killer?
- Does consistently overloading your workday enhance or kill productivity?
- Is multitasking a productivity enhancer or productivity killer?
- Is being plugged-in and accessible 24/7 a productivity enhancer or productivity killer?
- Is busyness good or bad for business?
- Does allowing or encouraging an intra-company "us versus them" attitude enhance or kill productivity?
- Does skipping or working through lunch every day, or not taking your vacation days, enhance your productivity or kill it?
- Does cutting back on training, because everyone is too busy to go to a class, enhance or kill productivity?

If actions speak louder than words, most people these days must believe that all the above are productivity enhancers. These are activities you can easily observe in a typical workplace nowadays. As a matter of fact, these are the kind of things you might often hear smart people brag about doing. However, most experts – including neuroscientists – who take the time to seriously study human productivity, seem to think otherwise. They think that most people are totally unaware of how many wheelbarrows, so to speak, are going out of the gate right in front of their eyes because of their lack of awareness of what is really going on.

Now What?

Recognizing bad productivity habits and *increasing your awareness* of activities that diminish or enhance your productivity is the best first step to take if you want to improve your productivity.

Awareness, of course, is a mental process. When we encounter problems, most of us have been programmed to do something tangible or take physical action. We are not typically wired to simply respond by raising our awareness to solve a problem. We are an action-oriented society, often more interested in attacking problems quickly than taking the time to clearly define them and understand the root causes. I saw a cartoon years ago about a sheriff and his deputy. The sheriff called the deputy into his office and said, "Deputy, there's a dangerous criminal on the loose. I want you to shoot first and ask questions later!" The deputy pulled out his gun, shot the sheriff full of holes, and then said, "What does he look like?"

As you may have observed from the two stories at the beginning of this chapter, it pays to slow down a bit and heighten your sense of awareness when you are looking for issues that diminish productivity.

So as a practical matter, how do we go about raising our awareness of something? As it turns out, it helps to have some awareness of a pathway of nerve fibers beginning in the lower brain stem and extending into other areas of the brain. This netlike core of nerve pathways operates the human arousal system, and is often referred to as the reticular activating system. Since we are bombarded with sensory input all day long and would go crazy if we had to deal with all of it, the reticular activating system does two things. It serves as a constant filter to block the unimportant, and it also serves as a gateway to allow important sensory input through to the higher-order brain structures for mental processing. It is not as important that you know about the anatomy or location of the reticular activating system as it is that you know it exists, and understand that *you can influence it*. You can, in effect, program your reticular activating system and significantly increase the odds that your brain will pay attention to something that is important.

This leads to one of the most common recommendations among self-help books and courses. If it is important for you to pay attention to something and remember it, *put it in writing*. The physical act of putting something in writing helps program the reticular activating system to notice it. Once you write down what you want to notice, consider using these two main strategies for encoding anything into memory: repetition and emotional tagging. Using these two methods can increase your odds of success. You are more likely to notice and remember things that are brought to your attention on a repetitive basis and things that are emotionally significant to you.

You can use these tips to help accomplish much in life. However, let's use them in this chapter to help raise your level of awareness related to workplace illusions, especially illusions that destroy productivity. Stop the wheelbarrows from going out the front gate. By workplace illusion, I simply mean any activity that seems like the right thing to do (since many people are doing it) and feels like the right thing to do (since you may have been doing it for a long time), but somehow seems to get in the way of getting the job done. Examples that quickly come to mind include excessive meetings, excessive e-mail checking, and the activities listed previously in this chapter.

In the rest of this book we will explore many of these workplace illusions. For now, just get out a 3 x 5 index card and write down whatever reminds you of the main lesson of this chapter (keep it short and simple) and look at the card several times a day until you think the idea is sticking in your brain. For example, you might write:

Be aware and beware of workplace illusions!

Also come up with an emotional reason for encoding this into your memory and conscious awareness. For example, you might decide, "I'm not going to be the kind of person who brags about a habit that solid scientific research has proven to be stupid!"

Try this idea after reading each chapter. Put the main lesson you get out of the chapter on a single index card and look at it frequently until you no longer need the card to remember it.

By the way, if you ever take a job as a security guard and your boss tells you to be on the lookout for employee theft, pay close attention to any piece of company property going out the gate. It might save you a wheelbarrow full of troubles!

2
Trains, Brains and Other Interesting Things

What?

I guess at this point in my life, some would say I have gone completely "around the bend" or "over the edge" about this issue of living a more joyful and productive life. It is no longer just an area of interest for me. It is my career, my passion and pretty much all I want to do for the rest of my life. I believe that studying and teaching this body of knowledge is my true calling, and my fascination with this field continues to grow stronger each day.

If you study any topic diligently, sooner or later you begin to see fascinating connections and begin to understand how various strands of knowledge and snippets of information come together at a common point. When this starts to happen, you can't help but wonder about the unifying element of it all. You wonder, "Is there a central idea, concept or focal point that pulls it all together?"

So, is there a focal point or unifying element of being focused, getting organized, and living a more joyful and productive life? I'm beginning to think there is!

So What?

If you observe highly focused, organized and productive people, you can usually track their behavior to the same controlling source. It's as if you backed down the train tracks heading out of New York City until you arrived at their originating point. If you do this, sooner or later, you arrive at or near 42nd Street and Park Avenue – New York's Grand Central Terminal.

In similar fashion, if you back down the tracks leading to improved focus, organization and productivity, they take you to the Grand Central Terminal of human beings…the brain.

I often tell people who are struggling to get more done, "If you get your mind right, everything else will begin to easily fall into place." I suspect most people probably pass this off as a casual statement or consider it tired, worn-out advice. However, in my mind, there is no better advice I can offer. I have studied this topic for a long, long time. I am becoming more convinced that the human brain is the focal point that pulls everything together. Therefore, if you understand more about how the brain works, you will begin to uncover the true secrets of living a more joyful and productive life.

Now What?

A friend of mine recently bought a very expensive, very sophisticated new car. Right after he bought it, we jumped in his car and took a short ride. The car is the high-tech automotive equivalent of a thermos. It knows! Just as a thermos somehow magically knows to keep cold things cold and hot things hot, this car knows how to assess various situations and respond accordingly and appropriately. It has enough buttons, switches, bells, whistles, gadgets and features to keep a rocket scientist happy for quite some time. Fortunately, my friend is a maven with regard to such matters, and I am convinced he will learn to use all the technological wonders available in his new car. However, I imagine some people will buy a car just like my friend's and never learn to use a fraction of the gadgets. All the gadgets will be available, ready for use, but they will get little use out of them until they take the time to understand how these features work.

In a sense, this is a good metaphor for your brain. It also has a lot of interesting bells, whistles, gadgets and features. You increase your ability to take advantage of these wonderful features if you know more about how they work. Here are just a few examples:

- The brain has three separate systems that either work in harmony or compete for control over your behavior. One system is in control of your automatic functions such as breathing, heartbeat, temperature, metabolism, etc. A separate brain system controls your emotional functions. A third system controls your ability to think, control impulsive behavior and exercise sound judgment. Everything works best when the systems are in balance and working together. When you see someone who is focused, organized and productive, the three systems are operating in harmony. The best way to create balance among the three systems is to pace yourself properly (as opposed to overloading your systems with too much input) and simply think about what you are doing...when you are doing it. Another way of saying this is: Do one thing at a time! Somewhat rare behavior these days. The brain systems work together best when you focus on one thing at a time.

- When you begin to overload your brain systems by multitasking, rushing or operating under too much stress, your emotional brain (the limbic system) takes over and starts calling the shots. One part of your emotional brain (the amygdala) hijacks your nervous system and takes total control of your behavior. Although this can be a good thing at times (for example, if you find yourself being chased by a saber-toothed tiger), unlike a thermos, the emotional brain doesn't always know how to respond appropriately to incoming messages from your five senses. For example, when the incoming messages indicate a tiger is on your tail, every nonessential brain system that doesn't have a lot to do with running in the opposite direction is essentially shut down. One of the first systems to shut down is the thinking system of your brain (the neocortex). Your emotional brain basically says, "Don't think, run!" The good news is that we are not chased by tigers very often these days. The bad news is our brains don't know that. Anytime you operate under too much stress, the brain thinks a tiger is on your tail, and shuts down the thinking functions of your brain. In general, when the thinking functions of your brain are shut down, you default to your habits…good or bad.

- The moral of this story: If you are going to operate in a state of heightened emotions, you had better install some very good habits in your brain and nervous system to handle things important to you. That's why pilots, astronauts and military people drill on emergency procedures so much. When the amygdala hijacks their nervous systems, they can still function effectively. Therefore, forming good habits is the key to success in being more productive. Planners, file systems, electronic gadgets and gizmos only work if the proper habits are formed first.

- The brain also houses your memory system, which operates much like a sophisticated tape recorder. Unlike a regular tape recorder, the brain's memory system stores both facts and feelings. When things happen to you, a part of your brain (the hippocampus) records the facts related to what happened and another part (the amygdala, again) records the feelings associated with the facts. When a similar, not necessarily identical, set of facts occur in the future, your mental tape recorder is turned on and the recorded feelings resurface and strongly influence your behavior. For example, if your parents scared you as a child by saying, "Don't talk to strangers," a little too often with a little too much emotion, you may have trouble being a superstar salesperson as an adult. You've probably got a tape running that inhibits your ability to perform one of the most critical functions in sales...talking to strangers. Most people have strong tapes related to money, taking orders, giving orders, being assertive and other issues related to being a successful businessperson. Some of your tapes serve you well, some don't! Learning more about your tapes can be an enlightening and highly productive experience.

- Although people often compare the brain to a computer, it is really better to think of it more as a chemical factory. All instructions issued by the brain are carried out by chemicals called neurotransmitters. Therefore, what you eat, how much you exercise, how you breathe, and any-

> thing you do that alters the chemicals flowing through your brain can alter your behavior. Basically, the neurotransmitters running through your brain and nervous system fall into two categories: excitatory or inhibitory. So take a look at your current life speed and figure out if you need to slow down or speed up. Here's a hint: Learning how to breathe properly is a good use of your time if you want to influence neurotransmitters.

I could go on and on about how the brain, tapes, neurotransmitters and other factors influence behavior, but here's the main point: If you really want to experience quantum leaps in your ability to be more productive, learn a little more about how your brain works. Although this book is about a variety of topics related to improving productivity, we'll touch on some key issues related to the brain. When you understand more about how the brain works, you can actually begin to exercise some measure of control over it, especially when you are operating under stress. Otherwise, it controls you, and you'll wonder why you intended to do one thing…but did another thing entirely.

3
Recognizing a Good Idea

What?

In the 1800s, Dr. Ignaz Semmelweis, a young Hungarian fresh out of medical school accepted a position in the Vienna General Hospital. The hospital had two separate maternity clinics. One clinic served as a training facility for medical students, and the other was set up to train midwives. In addition to his regular duties, Dr. Semmelweis was an instructor in the medical students' maternity clinic.

During his training as a physician, Dr. Semmelweis spent almost 15 months learning specialized diagnostic and statistical methods. Perhaps because of this special training and his personal interest in statistics, he was puzzled about something called puerperal fever that killed an unacceptably high percentage of young women giving birth in hospitals. He began vigorously investigating the cause of the fever in spite of the strong objections voiced by his superiors. Since a mortality rate of 25 percent to 30 percent was common at the time in maternity hospitals, his superiors were convinced that the deaths were normal and non-preventable. They believed it was a total waste of time and effort to investigate the deaths. But Semmelweis persisted, especially after one of his best friends, Dr. Jakob Kolletschka, died of puerperal fever shortly after cutting his finger while performing an autopsy on a woman who died in the maternity clinic.

Semmelweis noticed that the mortality rate of the patients in the maternity clinic run by midwives was only around 2 percent. He was keenly aware of the fact that physicians assigned to his clinic, where the mortality rate was significantly higher, often left the autopsy room without washing their hands and went directly to the delivery room to perform patient examinations and deliver babies. Midwives in the other clinic, of course, did not perform autopsies. He put two-and-two together and, on a hunch, established a policy requiring all physicians to wash their hands with a chlorinated lime solution after performing autopsies. Most of the doctors considered the new policy unnecessary and burdensome, but they were student-physicians so they reluctantly complied. The mortality rate in Dr. Semmelweis' clinic quickly fell below 2 percent.

Was Dr. Semmelweis rewarded for his efforts? Not exactly! The hospital director, believing his leadership had been compromised by Semmelweis, eventually forced him out of the hospital for being a troublemaker.

Semmelweis eventually took a position at a hospital in Budapest and used his ideas to quickly cut the mortality rate to less than 1 percent. After successfully implementing his ideas in other hospitals and achieving similar positive results, he eventually published a book on his findings and circulated it among members of the established medical community all over Europe. His book was poorly received and soundly criticized by prominent members of the existing medical establishment. Some doctors were actually offended by the thought that their hands might be considered unclean. One prominent obstetrician supposedly stated, "Doctors are gentlemen, and gentlemen's hands are clean."

Dr. Semmelweis responded to his critics with extreme anger and highly confrontational behavior. He even called some prominent physicians who rejected his ideas murderers. He ultimately hurt his own cause with his rage, frustration and inability to effectively handle criticism and conflict. He eventually became so distressed by the conflict that he suffered a nervous breakdown and was committed to a mental institution where he was severely beaten by attendants. He was only 47 years old at the time of his death, which occurred just a few days after being admitted to the mental institution.

Years later, Louis Pasteur officially "discovered" germs and Joseph Lister developed proven methods to minimize infections among surgical patients (yes, Listerine was named after Joseph). Joseph Lister said, "Without Semmelweis, my achievements would be nothing."

So What?

Powerful ideas are often rejected because they seem too simple to be true. The story of Dr. Ignaz Semmelweis is loaded with life lessons. Here are two I want to emphasize:

- Be the kind of person who actively seeks simple, powerful ideas and solutions.
- Be open-minded enough to listen to other people's simple ideas, especially when they are supported by proven and measurable results.

Of course, it is easy to nod your head affirmatively and agree to do these two things. However, let's take things a step further and consider how to structure your thinking in a way that will help you recognize a good idea when you encounter one.

Now What?

What makes a simple, powerful idea simple and powerful? How do you recognize one? Here are four basic factors to consider:

> **Impact** – Will this idea have an immediate and strong, positive impact on something or somebody?
>
> **Implementation** – Is this idea easy to implement?
>
> **Time** – How much time will it take to implement this idea?
>
> **Cost** – How much will it cost to implement this idea?

Think about Semmelweis' idea. How does it hold up considering these four factors? Let's see, it saved countless lives, so it was clearly a high-impact idea. It seems easy enough to wash your hands, it takes little time to wash your hands, and it costs little or nothing to wash your hands. I'd say it clearly qualifies as a simple and powerful idea. It's hard to believe that it was so soundly rejected by so many prominent experts in the field, isn't it? And another thing to consider, those closest to and most involved with a work process can often tell you the best ways to improve the process…if they believe their ideas will not be rejected without due consideration.

Let's get practical. Make a list of the problems that seem to occur frequently in your work environment. Find the people who are closest to the work processes related to the problem. Ask them for their suggestions and listen to them! Then use the four-factor analysis above (and any other common sense factors) to see if you can uncover any Semmelweis-like solutions.

Einstein said, "Any fool can make things bigger, more complex, and more violent. It takes a touch of genius – and a lot of courage – to move in the opposite direction."

4
Overloading

What?

What if by simply drawing a line you could reduce the suffering and anguish of thousands and save lives in the process? Wouldn't you think it was a good idea?

In 1874, seafarer Samuel Plimsoll did just that. Plimsoll found a way to prevent ships from being overloaded and sinking under the weight of excess cargo. Literally thousands of lives were saved because Plimsoll Lines, indicating the maximum vessel load capacity, were painted on the side of ships. Given today's overloaded workplaces and lifestyles, we can learn a lot from Plimsoll's approach. We can learn to draw a line indicating our maximum capacity and prevent the negative effects of personal overloading. The Plimsoll Line is a 19th century solution to a 21st century problem.

So What?

Although overloading can enter your life in different forms, it typically creates the same kind of problems for the person or object being overloaded. *Overloading creates a burden that is too great to bear and the consequences of that excessive burden negatively impact your life.* That is as true today as it was in the 1800s.

You might think we are the first generation to find ourselves trapped in this overloading dilemma, but history tells us otherwise. Overloading was actually a much more serious problem in earlier times. Rather than being a matter of getting smoothly through the day or coping with stress-inducing technology, overloading was literally a matter of life and death. This was especially true in the world of shipping.

When it comes to matters of staying afloat, a brief review of Archimedes' principle is in order. Archimedes discovered that a body immersed in a fluid is buoyed up by a force equal to the weight of the displaced fluid. Apply this to the world of shipping, and the consequences of overloading are clear. Ships sink when they weigh more than the water they displace. Ships will actually float at different levels depending on water temperature and type. Therefore, a ship loaded to capacity in a North Atlantic saltwater port would be in danger of riding too low and possibly sinking in a freshwater port in the tropics.

In earlier times, with only hand tools for the job, it took years to build a ship. Moving only under the power of wind and sails, it took months or years to sail across the sea and return. It made sense that ship owners and sailors would take extra precautions to assure the safety of their vessels. Unfortunately, ship owners did not always care. Why? As seafaring commerce developed, insurance coverage on the ships and cargo underwritten by such entities as Lloyd's of London often enticed ship owners to overload their ships. If the ships arrived safely, the payoff was greater for the more heavily loaded ships. If the ships sank, insurance covered the loss.

Also, in the mid-19th century the Irish potato famine reached its peak. Irish land owners, eager to shift their focus from potatoes to wheat and livestock, looked for ways to clear their land of Irish paupers made destitute due to the devastation of the potato crop. Landlords either evicted paupers with no promise of support, or packed them into unseaworthy vessels with phony promises of assistance in British North America, sending them out to sea. You can probably guess why these overloaded vessels were known as coffin ships. Many people lost their lives on these dangerous voyages. Eventually the general public became concerned enough about the loss of crafts, crew and passengers that British Parliament was forced to appoint a committee to investigate the growing number of sinking ships.

Enter Samuel Plimsoll. As a young man Plimsoll was fascinated with the problems of shipping coal to London. The main problem that attracted his attention was the simple fact that too many ships were sinking. In 1868, Plimsoll was elected a member of British Parliament. He immediately began to campaign for legislation to protect seamen. In 1873, he published a book titled *Our Seamen* that documented the fact that every year nearly 1,000 sailors drowned on ships near and around the British shores. These numbers did not include casualties from British ships that sank in locations other than the British coastline. Fishing vessels were excluded from this total and so were non-British ships that sunk.

Plimsoll's solution was simple: determine the maximum safe load a vessel could handle and make sure the vessel never exceeded that load. He proposed that a mark or line be painted on the side of all ships to indicate the limit to which the vessel could be legally loaded. If the weight and buoyancy of the ship caused it to dip below the line – referred to as the Plimsoll Mark or Plimsoll Line – the ship could not set sail. The Merchant Shipping Act of 1876 made these load lines compulsory.

Unfortunately, the line's actual position was not fixed by the 1876 law. As might be expected, the ship owners loosely interpreted the law and painted the line wherever they wanted, until the position was finally fixed by another law passed in 1894. It is estimated that this simple line has saved countless lives since the late 1800s.

Now What?

So here we are at the beginning of the 21st century. Many of us live nowhere near the sea. What can we learn from the Plimsoll Line story that will make our lives better?

Acknowledge that *consistently* overloading yourself is a form of dysfunctional behavior driven by irrational thinking. Therapists usually embrace one of two approaches when trying to help their clients solve such behavioral problems. They focus on the past so their clients can understand more about the source of their behavior, or they tell their clients to "forget the past" and work mainly on changing the unproductive behavior going forward. Here are examples of each of these approaches that you might consider trying:

- By studying the history of shipping in the 1800s, Samuel Plimsoll began to understand why so many ships were sinking and developed a simple solution to the problem of overloading. If you are struggling with problems related to overloading, it is a good idea to study your personal history and discover past events and decisions that led to your present dilemma. One bad habit or decision rarely creates an overload of demands on your time and energy. It is usually a combination of many decisions and patterns of behavior. For example, people-pleasing behavior, and the inability to say "no" when it is appropriate, can create overloading. Study your personal history and see if you can identify specific decisions that are creating an excessive workload. I know this strategy sounds a bit oversimplified (somewhat like drawing a line on the side of ships and saving countless lives), but here's an idea for you: Stop making those same decisions if you want to eliminate overloading in the future.

- Forget the past and just experiment until you discover your personal Plimsoll Line. Make a commitment to work no more than eight hours most days. You are kidding yourself if you think working 12, 14, 16 or more hours per day is a productive use of your time. Doing this sounds impressive to some people, but not to those who understand how the various systems of the human body work to optimize your performance. Your productivity plummets when you exceed your optimal workload. You will eventually sink. Try breaking an eight-hour day into 48-minute segments (there are, of course, 10 of these segments available). Make a commitment to spend at least 48 uninterrupted minutes tomorrow working on the most important things you need, want, or have to do to be successful. Then operate in your normal manner for the rest of the day. The next day go for two 48-minute blocks of highly focused time. My suggestion is that you draw your Plimsoll Line at about three 48-minute blocks of focused time most days. I am not suggesting that you only work 144 minutes each day. I am simply suggesting that you mentally designate three highly focused periods in a workday as a highly successful day. Then, cut yourself a little slack and stop pushing yourself so hard.

In the end remember that overloading is an upstream problem. When the ships began sinking in the warm freshwater due to being overloaded in the cold saltwater ports, it was a little late to start working on a solution to the problem. It would have been better to prevent the problems before the ships embarked on the voyage. The upstream issue that leads to work overload is making the decision to take on any additional tasks. If you are already overloaded, start focusing on how to eliminate tasks, not increase them. Start making sound decisions today to prevent overloading in the future.

5
Dealing With Devious Traffic-Flow Designers

What?

I don't know much about traffic light timing. However, I suspect that a mischievous traffic-flow designer is having a bit of fun at the expense of lead-footed drivers in my hometown. On one particular stretch of road, the timing of the lights and the inevitable consequences of hastily accelerating and exceeding the speed limit between any two given traffic lights seems way too predictable to be a coincidence. No matter how fast you accelerate after a light turns green, you will not make it to the next light before it turns red. It would not surprise me to see the devious traffic-flow designer sitting near an intersection at noon, eating his lunch out of a paper bag, and chuckling at the fools who attempt to challenge and overcome his precisely coordinated traffic lights.

On this particular road, the traffic lights are spaced just far enough apart to encourage unsuspecting people to gun it, go for it, and try to make the next light before it turns red. I doubt if the sinister traffic-flow designer has much to do with the spacing between intersections. However, he does apparently use the same mathematics to synchronize the traffic lights on this stretch of road that statisticians use to stack the odds in favor of the house in Las Vegas casinos. Gamblers and speeding citizens are no match for these mathematically gifted designers. Fortunately I recognized the workings of an evil mind after a few stop-and-start trips down this road.

So What?

Once I realized what was going on, I decided to play a game I call "Tortoise and Hare – Peripheral Vision Roadway Edition," with my traffic mates when I drive along this road. Admittedly the game is shameless, but it helps reinforce my beliefs related to the importance of pacing yourself properly at work. It also gives me something to do on this road rather than getting frustrated with the poorly coordinated traffic lights. Here's how the game is played:

- The game is best played when you and another potential player are alone at a traffic light, side by side, and waiting for the signal to change to green. Make no direct eye contact with the potential player at this time.

- As you wait for the light to change, lightly release your brakes and "inadvertently" inch forward a few times. Move forward enough to allow the potential player to pick up on the movement with his peripheral vision. Make no direct eye contact with the potential player at this time.

- When the light turns green, if the potential player guns it and rockets forward, the game is on! You have identified and engaged a player.

- Slowly drive away from the traffic light and accelerate smoothly. There is no hurry. Mathematics, timing, and the devious traffic-flow designer are on your side. At the next intersection, pull up beside the other player and repeat the process. Make no direct eye contact with the other player at this time.

- When you roll up slowly at the third or fourth intersection, make casual eye contact with the other player and smile pleasantly. Congratulations! The game is over…you win! The other player has burned more gas, worn out more tires and brake pads, and put much more wear and tear on his vehicle. You, on the other hand, have made just as much forward progress without the accompanying frustration and wear and tear on your vehicle. At this point, the other player will likely be in an agitated state, so make sure your smile is very subtle or understated. At the mastery level, the other player should never be quite sure that you are actually playing a game. For extra points, wait until the other player jackrabbits away from the intersection and then look around to see if you can locate a person who appears to be a governmental bureaucrat eating his lunch from a paper bag. If you spot one, point at him and give him a thumbs-up, or maybe even a Tiger Woods' fist pump.

Now What?

You will probably get a lot out of this story if you understand it illustrates the value of pacing yourself properly in the workplace. Especially if thoughts such as the following flashed through your mind as you read it:

- I wonder how often the jackrabbit player has to replace the brakes on his car.

- I wonder how this stop-and-start driving is influencing his gas mileage.

- I wonder how many intersections it will take for the other player to figure things out.

- I wonder if the race from light to light, with little forward progress, could represent a typical workday for many people.

- I wonder if the increased wear and tear could represent what happens to many people who frantically race from place to place in a typical work environment.

- I wonder what other parallels exist between the elements of this story and events in the workplace.

You probably need to forget about this book for now if you read the story and thought, "I'll bet I could make a lot of those damn lights!"

Look around! How many people are playing the equivalent of the traffic light game in the workplace? Is it helping or hurting their performance and productivity? Learn to appropriately pace yourself at work. It makes a lot of sense in the long run.

6
Racing and Pacing

What?

Would you pull in for a pit stop?

Imagine you have been totally focused on driving as fast as possible around a 2.5 mile racetrack for almost three hours. So far, you have averaged more than 175 mph. You are out in front of the other drivers and have a 23-second lead on your next closest competitor. You know that this lead means you are slightly more than a mile ahead of the drivers trying to catch you. You also know that your gas tank holds exactly 22 gallons, and the car you are driving typically gets between 4 and 6 miles per gallon (usually closer to 4 than 6). Your last pit stop was 41 laps ago and you now have only four laps to go. There is no guarantee, but if all goes well, a pit stop at this point would probably take 16 seconds or less. Everyone else among the leaders made pit stops to refuel eight or nine laps ago. Your closest competitor got in and out of the pits in 6.3 seconds! At this point you know for sure you are getting more than 4 mpg, otherwise, you would have run out of gas about six laps ago. It's going to be close! If you are getting even slightly more than 5 mpg, you can make it to the finish line without a pit stop. The mathematics in favor of making a pit stop looks promising. You can pull in for gas, get back on the track, and probably still maintain a slight lead. But pit stop times are not guaranteed. All kinds of things can go wrong, and a few extra seconds in the pits might be the difference between a win and a loss. The mathematics in favor of fuel consumption is less promising. However, at the speed you are traveling, you only have to keep going for three or four more minutes to win the race. What would you do? Would you pull in and get gas, or would you take a chance and go for it?

So What?

How counterintuitive do you think it would feel to slow down even a bit, much less go from more than 175 mph to a complete stop with only four laps to go? Forget about mathematics and logic for a minute. Use your imagination and tap into *how it must feel* to be in such an intense situation. Slowing down or stopping will not likely feel like the right thing to do. It will simply not feel natural. Many people face a similar dilemma at work every day. Their workday unfolds like a race. They race from meeting to meeting, project to project, task to task, and value speed and quantity over proper pacing and quality. However, there is one big difference. There never seems to be a finish line. At least the racecar driver knows it will be over one way or another, in three or four minutes.

I didn't make up this racing scenario. Geoff Bodine, the leader of the 1987 Daytona 500, found himself in this position with four laps to go. He chose to take a chance and keep going. His engine sputtered with three laps to go and he was forced to roll slowly to the inside lane of the track as the rest of the drivers roared past him. He gambled and lost!

After the fact, it is easy to see that skipping the pit stop was not a good gamble. Bodine was a seasoned professional. He knew that the typical car in such a race would probably average about 4.5 mpg. That means a 22-gallon gas tank was good for about 99 miles. He knew that with four laps to go, he had already squeezed more than 102 miles out of the tank of fuel from the pit stop 41 laps ago. Maybe in the heat of battle Bodine wasn't thinking about the precise mathematics of fuel consumption (although I doubt that), but you can bet someone in his pit crew was wearing out a calculator and warning Bodine that things weren't looking so good. Here's what happened: he was human. It felt totally counterintuitive to stop and it felt totally right to keep going! Maybe things are not quite as intense in the typical workplace, but whatever kept Bodine going when he should have stopped also keeps busy, stressed, overloaded people going at work when they should probably stop.

Now What?

Make the decision to pace yourself at work and stop trying to squeeze a few more miles out of an empty tank. *Stop confusing frenetic motion with constructive action.* That's the advice of Heike Bruch and Sumantra Ghoshal in a very interesting article they published in the *Harvard Business Review* titled "Beware the Busy Manager" (February 2002, p. 5-11). In this article they posed the question, "Are the least effective executives the ones who look like they are doing the most?" After reading the article, I would say the answer is a resounding, "Yes!"

Think about why it feels so counterintuitive to slow down and operate at a reasonable pace. You didn't come into the world with a "don't make any pit stops" attitude. You learned it somewhere along the way. Near the end of his fascinating book, *Brain Rules,* author and brain research specialist John Medina relates a story about walking down the street with his two-year old son.

Because of his son's curiosity, it took them 15 minutes to walk 20 feet. Medina's first reaction was to try and get his son to move along and "act like an adult with a schedule." Because of Medina's knowledge of the value of nurturing curiosity, he decided to go along with the 15-feet-per-20-minute pace his son had set for them. On that day, he decided *not* to teach his son that speed is always best, or that a person's value as a human is directly related to the speed at which they operate.

Don't get me wrong. There is a time and a place for everything, including picking up the pace and staying on a schedule. However, no matter how busy you are due to the circumstances of your life, always remember to make periodic pit stops to restore your energy and allow for the repair and replacement of worn parts. Learn to properly pace yourself! *When you least feel like slowing down or stopping, you probably most need to do so.* Awareness is the key issue. Make the decision to value pace and quality over speed and quantity.

7
Do You Want to Avoid Getting Whacked?

What?

I recently read something interesting in a book titled *The Biology of Belief* by Bruce H. Lipton, Ph.D. In the chapter titled "Growth and Protection," Dr. Lipton discusses how the human body generates and uses energy. Lipton is a cell biologist and for some reason, his comments about allocating energy to the various growth and protection systems of the body reminded me of the game Whac-A-Mole. Whac-A-Mole is a simple game. Moles constantly pop up through holes and you whack them with a mallet. Unfortunately, there are several holes, many moles and only one mallet.

So What?

So what does playing Whac-A-Mole have to do with human energy use? Imagine that whacking a mole with a mallet symbolizes how we respond to a request for energy. After all, it takes energy to swing a mallet and whack a mole. According to Dr. Lipton, there are four major growth and protection systems, or energy-using moles, that may pop up and need to be whacked at times. The body needs energy for:

- The sympathetic "fight or flight" nervous system (to deal with real or perceived external threats)
- The immune system (to deal with internal threats, viruses, bacteria, etc.)
- The cell replacement system (body cells constantly wear out and need to be replaced)
- The energy replacement system (it takes energy to run all the body systems, including the system that generates energy)

Just as you only have one mallet in Whac-A-Mole, you only have so much energy to allocate to these various systems. You just can't whack them all at the same time! Therefore, if one system is drawing too much energy, the other systems cannot do their jobs. This, in my mind, is a good explanation of how stress can kill you. Or as Tony Soprano might say, whack you. Think about it. If you constantly operate in a stressful environment and your fight or flight mole needs constant whacking, there is not enough energy left over to fight off internal threats, replace worn out cells and generate new energy. It's the human body's version of a deadly zero-sum game. Keep rushing around, multitasking, overloading, under-relaxing, and all the other stress generating activities, and you will eventually whack yourself. Yes, we all need some stress to function properly. But we don't need to play Whac-A-Mole with our lives. I don't know about you, but I want my immune, cell replacement, and energy replacement systems to have all the energy they need to do their jobs.

It's important to remember that the fight or flight system will take whatever energy it needs to deal with external threats – real or perceived – with or without your approval. Any remaining energy will be allocated to the other systems. So in order to have enough energy for all systems to function properly, you must consciously place a high priority on activities that restore your energy.

Now What?

What energizes you? Most activities fall into one of two broad categories: activities that increase your energy and activities that drain your energy. Most people also fall into the same two categories. Make a conscious and ongoing effort to participate in energy-generating activities, and hang around energy-generating people (limit your time spent with drama kings and queens).

Identify your energy restoring activities. You can't participate in them if you do not know what they are. Maybe for you it is fishing, playing a musical instrument, gardening or painting. In all likelihood, you can simply resurrect an old hobby you abandoned when your life became so hectic. If you need help coming up with a hobby, go to the Wikipedia Web site, look up "List of Hobbies" and see if anything appeals to you. Maybe you can combine several of the hobbies. For example, you can very nicely combine bird watching and photography. FYI…I noticed nudism and blacksmithing are both on the list. You might want to avoid combining these hobbies. Once you identify a good hobby or energy-restoring activity, treat it just as you would a high work priority. Devote some time to your new hobby (or resurrected hobby) each week. Schedule this time just as you would schedule time with your boss, a staff member, customer, prospect, etc. Use this time to create enough energy to enable all your life-prolonging systems to do what they do best. In other words, quit trying to whack yourself!

8
The Multitasking Illusion

What?

If you want to think more clearly, exercise more control over impulsive behavior, make better decisions and improve your day-to-day productivity, *stop accepting the false premise that you can multitask and that multitasking is a positive human attribute.* The truth is multitasking is highly unproductive and at times outright rude. People who like to brag about being multitaskers, especially those who believe it is appropriate to take several calls or check their messages while they are interacting with you, should probably be apologizing for it rather than bragging about it.

What we commonly think of as multitasking has much in common with motion pictures. Both the sensation that you are multitasking at work and the "motion" in motion pictures are illusions. When you observe someone who is supposedly multitasking, it usually looks as if many things are going on simultaneously. However, the activities you observe are not occurring at the same time. What you are actually seeing is a rapid series of stop/start/stop/start actions. In a way, it is similar to watching a movie. It certainly looks as if things on the screen are moving. However, you are actually viewing a rapid series of still pictures that create the illusion of movement. The human eye apparently perceives typical cinema film motion as being fluid at about 18 or more frames per second. In a darkened theater with a reflective screen, the motion you think you detect is actually created by exposing a rapid series of about 24 still pictures per second to your visual sensory systems.

Take a moment and try to talk with someone on the phone (or listen to a voice mail) and read and respond to an e-mail simultaneously. Pay very close attention to what is actually going on and *how you feel* as you switch your attention back and forth among the various activities. If you are honest with yourself, you will realize that you are not really multitasking, you are nano-flipping your attention between the activities.

I enjoy reading biographies about prominent people and high achievers. I always look for common traits among these people – things they do differently from others. One of the traits that comes up often and seems to make a significant difference is how these people interact with others. You often discover that people who are widely admired are highly focused when interacting with others. They make appropriate eye contact. They listen attentively and give others their full and undivided attention during a personal interaction. How would you like interacting with such a person? How would you like to be such a person? At a minimum, when you are interacting with other humans, forget multitasking and become a unitasker. If you try this, I suspect you will notice an immediate improvement in your personal relationships.

So What?

I'll lighten up a bit and tell you that occasionally trying to juggle things and keep a lot of balls in the air is relatively harmless.

That's the reality of modern life for most people. However, when juggling becomes your *preferred and ongoing* method of operating, it can destroy your productivity and peace of mind.

Let's look at multitasking from the brain's point of view. Parts of the brain – the older and lesser evolved structures, such as the brain stem (often referred to as the primitive brain) – are actually designed to multitask. They maintain basic life-sustaining functions such as breathing, heart rate, digestive processes and body temperature. All of these functions go on simultaneously without any conscious effort on your part. You don't have to think about them. However, if you must think about a task, it must be handled by the newer, and more evolved, structures of the brain such as the prefrontal cortex (often referred to as the executive brain or thinking brain). Whereas the primitive brain is designed to handle multiple functions simultaneously, the thinking brain is simply not designed to do so. Therefore, if sensory input related to two separate thinking tasks (such as talking on the phone and sending an e-mail) start their journey through the neural pathways of your brain en route to the prefrontal cortex for processing, sensory input related to one of the tasks is *going to be blocked by certain brain structures and, in effect, told to wait in line.* That is because the brain also has structures designed to filter *most* incoming sensory information. Otherwise, you would go nuts from sensory overload. All this happens so fast it seems as if you are multitasking when, in fact, you are nano-flipping your attention.

What happens when two, three or more neural pathways get activated at about the same time? Let's keep looking at things from the brain's point of view. The human brain is no slouch. It's going to try its best to handle all the items. It just can't override this "pay attention to one thing at a time" feature built into the structures and systems that process sensory input. The brain's attempt to handle multiple tasks ultimately destroys productivity. *Each separate task has a set of mental processing rules related to performing the task.* For example, the mental processing rules for handing a phone call are different than the mental processing rules for handling an e-mail. When you nano-flip between or among tasks, you must mentally put away the rules for the old task and retrieve the rules for the new task. All this shuffling between tasks, and the rules governing the performance of the tasks, creates significant ramp-up and ramp-down time. And this ramp-up and ramp-down time severely diminishes productivity.

Now What?

The bottom line: Doing one thing at a time, or unitasking, is almost always a better idea than multitasking. I agree that this seems a bit counterintuitive, but that's what illusions are all about. Illusions trick you into believing something that is not true. Illusions cannot survive in the presence of reality. And reality dictates that the thinking structures of the brain are designed to handle one thing at a time.

Now forget all this brain stuff for a moment and think about the reality of working on one thing at a time versus multitasking. Which is better in terms of productivity, enjoyment and peace of mind? These are three pretty good criteria for choosing a preferred mode of operation. Imagine a time when you were extremely focused and stayed with a task from beginning to closure. How did things go in terms of these three measures of success? How productive were you? How enjoyable was the task? How would you rate your peace of mind during and after completing the task?

You didn't come into the world as a multitasker. You had to learn to do it somewhere along the way. Maybe it is time to learn to unitask. Who is the most important person in your life? Start unitasking when you are interacting with him or her. See how you like it. Hopefully you will enjoy it so much you will decide to expand it to other areas of your life.

9
The Big Three

What?

Allow me to get a bit Joyce Kilmer-ish for a moment: "I think that I shall never see, a *number* as beautiful as a 3."

I don't think Joyce would mind me borrowing a line from his poem about trees to help introduce the idea that the number "3" is important to people who feel overwhelmed. Three is a useful number if you are a busy person, a digestible number…it's anti-overwhelming. Three has long been an important number among religious teachers and public speakers. It is important in the fields of art and entertainment, and it is important to people who are struggling with their workload.

My friend, who is a retired minister, told me that he was taught in seminary to design sermons using the "three points and a poem" format. Great speakers have long known the value of writing speeches with three main points. And many movies, TV sitcoms and plays use a three-part or three-act story line format. *Seinfield* often launched three stories in the beginning of each episode and tied them all together by the end of the show. And of course, there are the Three Bears, the Three Little Pigs, the Three Stooges, the Three Musketeers, the Three Blind Mice, the

Three Laws of Robotics (if you are a science-fiction and Isaac Asimov fan), and then there's the big three in school: reading, writing and arithmetic. The list goes on and on...and on.

In terms of triage, the medical practice of properly categorizing incoming patients in a massive emergency when the number of patients needing attention exceeds lifesaving resources, the number 3 has the potential to save your life. There are many forms of triage that vary slightly. For purposes of this discussion, let's assume the triage physician has been taught to categorize incoming patients as follows:

1. Will not survive even if treated immediately.
2. Will survive even if not treated immediately.
3. Will only survive if treated immediately.

In case you haven't already guessed, here's where I am going with all this talk about the number 3. Frequently perform triage on your workload. Design most of your days so you will complete the three most important things you need to get done each day before noon.

So What?

Let's talk about the simple psychology related to this strategy. Using this triage technique makes it much easier to decide what to do next. If you have a multitude of things on your mind and a work environment full of projects circling your desk waiting to land, you can easily succumb to the negative effects of choice overload. Here's a relevant quote from Barry Schwartz, author of the book *The Paradox of Choice*:

> *"As the number of available choices increases, as it has in our consumer culture, the autonomy, control, and liberation this variety brings are powerful and positive. But as the number of choices keeps growing, negative aspects of having a multitude of options begins to appear. As the number of choices grows further, the negatives escalate until we become overloaded. At this point, choice no longer liberates, but debilitates. It might even be said to tyrannize."*

Barry's comments also apply to you and your workload. You can become debilitated by choice overload whether you are trying to buy a new pair of jeans, a camera or a car, or trying to decide what to do next at work.

Now What?

Use the triage technique to schedule your morning activities and then shift down one more gear into a binary decision-making mode (the opposite of choice overload). The term binary means "consisting of two parts or two separate elements." If it is before noon, you simply compare any potential distraction – e-mails, phone calls, drop-in visitors, etc. – with the most important unfinished item on your list of the three important things to get done for the day. It is much easier to compare competing demands for your time and make a decision if you are comparing two things, rather than trying to constantly juggle a multitude of things. This process also allows for the fact that something may come up that is more important than any of the three things you previously thought were the most important. If that should happen, ignore the original three items until you complete the unexpected important task. Only become concerned about doing this if you begin to notice a pattern of frequent, unexpected items. Repeat the process in the afternoon or work in a totally unstructured manner. Do whatever works best for you. I personally think there is a lot of value in having plenty of unstructured time.

Consider setting up a triage hanging file in your desk drawer. Take three minutes at the end of each day to jot down the three most important things you have to do the next day, and then drop the list of three items into the triage file and go home.

You may think getting three things done each day is a bit wimpy. However, I didn't say you only had to do three things a day. I am simply suggesting that, at a minimum, you get three very important things done each day before you allow other less important forces to take control of your behavior. Ideally, by concentrating, focusing and minimizing distractions early in the day, you will finish your triage items and have plenty of time to continue your focused efforts. Or, you can join the masses in the world of the overwhelmed, if that is your preference.

I'll admit, when I get my triage items done some days, I like to screw around awhile and piddle with the work equivalent of shiny objects that attract my attention. However, I find that if I am honest and rational about what I put on my triage list, I feel very good about what I accomplish most days. For example, I am almost finished writing this chapter and it's not even time for lunch yet. Finishing this chapter ended up on my triage list since one of the roles I have defined for myself is being an author.

This brings up another important issue related to joyful and productive living. Maintain a long-term vision and a short-term focus. My long-term vision is to publish and sell books. My short-term focus related to this vision is to write one thing at a time and turn it over to my publisher to see if she can turn it into something with a cover, pages and a price tag. This short-term focus stuff won't work as well if you don't have a clue about your long-term vision.

In a way, writers are lucky. When you define yourself as a writer, your long-term vision and short-term focus are easy to determine. Writers write. If you don't write most days, you are probably not really a writer. Now that I think about it, it is probably a pretty good idea to see if you can come up with a one-word description of your main focus. That would mean that sellers sell, managers manage, leaders lead, teachers teach, inventors invent, and so forth and so on. Using sellers as an example doesn't mean they sell all the time. However, it does mean they sell most of the time and, hopefully, they sell some each day. It also means that activities related to selling should be the kind of items most frequently dropped in their triage file.

I know life is not always this simple, but keeping things simple is a good idea when you are trying to establish a reasonable level of order in your life. In reality, some days I am a teacher and items related to teaching belong in my triage file. Some days I am a vacationing spouse and parent. On those days, items related to watching the sunset from the beach, eating shrimp, and taking my daughter to get Hawaiian Shaved Ice belong in my triage file. Life balance is the ultimate trump card when considering your triage list.

That's all for now on this topic. Admit it, some of you didn't know Joyce Kilmer was a guy, did you?

10
Hitting the Sweet Spot at Work

What?

Golf clubs, rackets, bats and other devices used to hit sporting balls have what is referred to as a sweet spot. I don't really know how to explain the physics of a sweet spot. I suspect most of you already know exactly what it means. If you don't, go to a driving range and swing at golf balls long enough and eventually you will hear and feel it. When you hit the ball with the sweet spot of the club, it sounds and feels different than hitting the ball with any other part of the clubface. You'll hear a nice clean-sounding click or ping and feel the sensation of the ball effortlessly springing off the clubface. It's what most golfers do occasionally (usually on the last hole, right before giving up the stupid game of golf for good) and Tiger does almost every time. I guess the best way to describe hitting a ball on the sweet spot of the club, racket or bat is to say, "You'll know it when you feel it." And that's the best way to determine the sweet spot at work…you'll know it when you feel it!

So What?

You determine your personal work sweet spot by adjusting two things: your workload and the level of challenge related to the tasks you perform on a regular basis. In the long run, people do their best work when their chances of success are 50/50. Think about it. If you sail through your workday with ease, it probably won't be long before you become bored. Taking on brutal challenges day in and day out sounds noble and courageous, but it's a proven formula for generating excess stress and anxiety. So how do you feel the sweet spot at work? It's the feeling between boredom and anxiety. If boredom is creeping into your day, pick up the pace. Look for more challenging things to do. If too many of your days are filled with excess stress and anxiety, accept the reality of the situation, and at least temporarily adjust your challenges.

Now What?

Let's see if we can find your work sweet spot. Block out one week for sweet-spot-finding. I'm not suggesting that you goof off this week. To the contrary, I want you to make this a highly productive week at the same time you are finding your sweet spot. Follow the guidelines below for one week and don't cheat:

- Day 1 (first 30 minutes) – Take up to the first half-hour of your day listing everything you *must* get done this week. Hopefully this should only take you five minutes. However, take whatever time it takes (up to a half-hour) to put some serious thought into this and do a good job. Before you start making your list, look up the word "must" in the dictionary. Only list things you absolutely must do. If you have been operating under a lot of stress, simply making this list should make you feel a bit better.

- Day 1 (second 30 minutes) – Select the three most important items from your list. Make sure you can complete any item selected in one hour or less of focused work time. If a huge time-consuming project is the most important item on your list, break it up into the first (or next) step that you can complete in less than one hour. Or you can combine four 15-minute tasks and consider them a one hour-long project. Use any method you'd like to come up with 60 minutes worth of work.

- Day 1 (second hour) – *Kill the first project on your list!* Back in my days as a CPA, we used to talk about "killing" a project. I know one interpretation of this might be to cancel a project, but that's not what we meant. When someone advised you to kill a project, or you advised someone to kill a project, it meant *get it done, right now, without further delay, make it happen, don't screw around, do what it takes, focus, focus, focus*. Stuff like that!

- Day 1 (third hour) – *Kill the second project on your list!*

- Day 1 (fourth hour) – Do whatever it takes to deal with all the less important stuff that has come up in the first three hours of the day.

- Day 1 (lunch) – Do whatever you want.

- Day 1 (the first hour after lunch) – *Absolutely kill the third project on your list!*

- Day 1 (second hour after lunch) – Stop and determine how you feel in terms of your stress and anxiety level. If you feel fine, go to the next item on your list and work on it at whatever pace suits you. Tomorrow, go for four kills before letting up. If you feel overly stressed, back off a bit and try for two kills tomorrow.

- Day 2 to 5 – Adjust your workload up and down until you feel you are hitting your sweet spot at work.

If after one week, you have not found your optimal workload in terms of one-hour projects killed per day, you are going to have to face the fact that you may be in over your head (your work challenges might be in excess of your current skills). No one wants to personally admit this. It is human nature to deny the fact that such a thing could ever happen. The good news, by learning to kill projects, you'll probably free up adequate time to deal with this issue on your own before your boss or Mother Nature steps in and takes care of it for you. By the way, no matter how high you feel you can push your daily kill rate, always leave at least two hours of every workday unscheduled. You know…stuff happens! If you fill your kill quota for the day and nothing else has come up, go play golf, tennis or hit balls with a bat.

11
Accepting the Inflexibility of Time

What?

Do you know what happens 9,192,631,770 times a second? No, it's not the number of times your children ask, "Are we there yet?" when you are driving to your vacation destination.

I'll give you a hint. It has to do with the most accurate calculation of time known to man. In 1967, attendees of the 13th General Conference of Weights and Measurement reversed a long-standing tradition and redefined how we measure seconds. They decided to use atomic time rather than the motion of the Earth to measure the passage of one second. The standard second is now defined as 9,192,631,770 cycles of the natural frequency of certain cesium atoms (whatever that means). Stick with me for a few billion cycles of a cesium atom and I'll explain what all this talk about accurately measuring time has to do with one of the primary complaints among people who want be more productive.

Cesium-based atomic clocks measure and set the standard for time so accurately that they supposedly vary only one second in 1.4 billion years. Therefore, measuring time is one of the most stable and predictable things in your life. I am not saying there are *no* adjustments to or variations in time. Since scientists like to keep their atomic clocks in sync with what we non-scientists think of as a day (in terms of the rotation of the Earth, sunlight and darkness and that kind of stuff), they occasionally make slight adjustments to their sophisticated clocks. For example, every so often scientists add one second to our year just to keep things in sync. This process gives new meaning to the statement, "Hey, have you got a second?" Things must have gotten way out of whack in 1972 because they added two seconds to that year. Since the two-second adjustment in 1972, they have added a total of 21 seconds to their fancy atomic clocks.

So What?

At this point, you may be wondering why I bothered telling you so much about measuring time. It is because I hope the story about measuring time will help you take the first step in solving a problem that people encounter quite often in their quest to live more productive lives. Simply stated, people run out of day before they run out of things to do. The No. 1 complaint I hear among people who want to be more productive is, "I don't have time to get everything done!" I realize it's human nature to say something like that when you are under stress and overloaded, and not really mean it literally. However, when and if you really are overloaded and genuinely desire to address the issue, the first step in solving the problem is facing the fact that *the amount of time in a day is relatively unchangeable* (give or take a couple of seconds) and *adjusting to that reality.*

Now What?

Accept and adjust to the fact that each day of your life will likely be made up of 86,400 seconds, 86,401 seconds or 86,402 seconds. Henry Kissinger once said, "The absence of alternatives clears the mind marvelously." It has been my observation that many problems related to productivity must be solved in the mind first. Take your age and subtract zero from it. That's how long you have already had to adjust to the fact that you will only have so many seconds in a day. People who haven't mentally accepted this reality continue to try and pack too many activities in a day and then complain about not having enough time to get everything done. I would think at some point it would become a bit embarrassing to admit that you are so out of touch with reality.

As I write this, the presidential campaign is fully underway. It has been interesting to watch the candidates go all out in their efforts to become president of the United States. They hop around the country in an attempt to interact with and influence as many people as possible in a given day. It struck me that even though these are some of the most powerful people on Earth and they have access to huge sums of money…there is still nothing they can do about the fact that there are only 86,400 seconds in a day. They can try to schedule more than 86,400 seconds worth of activity in a day. However, it won't work any better for them than it will for you.

Here's the bottom line: Accepting the reality that there is a fixed quantity of time in a day is a great first step if you want to solve problems related to time shortage. My teenage daughter frequently says things I do not understand. When I ask her about them she says, "Dad, it's an inside joke." Let's develop an inside joke. Whenever someone says, "I don't have enough time to get everything done," silently think, "Isn't that odd! That person appears to be otherwise intelligent and in touch with reality. However, they are unaware of the fact that there is only so much time in a day. They still haven't learned that they are going to have *to adjust their workload* to solve their problem since the amount of time in a day is fixed. I wonder why they keep overloading their workday and setting themselves up for failure."

You can try to help them get in touch with reality if you feel like it. However, I suspect most people struggling with time shortage won't pay much attention to your advice. In the middle of their chaos, they are probably in the "not ready to hear" mode. Just use their comments to reinforce your belief that it is not a great idea to go around advertising that you are out of control and out of touch with reality.

I realize that this chapter does not require you to do anything other than make a simple mental adjustment. However, never discount the power of mental adjustments. In his book *As A Man Thinketh,* James Allen stated that "thoughts are the ancestors of all actions." Einstein advised that you can't solve problems using the same kind of thinking that created them in the first place. In other words, it is important to get your mind right first if you want to work your way out of a problem situation. Once you face reality, you will be in a much better position to roll up your sleeves and do something tangible to address the problem. For example, clear thinking people understand that there are four excellent options for adjusting their workload. They can:

- Eliminate low value tasks.
- Delegate activities to other people.
- Delegate activities to some form of technology.
- Explore efficiency solutions.

Each of these options, in turn, opens up multiple pathways for freeing up huge blocks of time. Get you mind right first, and stop trying to ignore reality.

12
Delegation Math

What?

Here's a quick idea if you are consistently overloaded at work. Have you ever said or heard anyone say, "Yes, I know I should delegate this task to someone else, but it will be easier to just do it myself." I'll buy into that philosophy if the task only has to be done once or twice. However, this statement makes no sense if you know the task will show up frequently in your life.

So What?

Do the math. Assume a weekly task typically takes you 20 minutes to complete. However, it will take you three hours to teach someone else how to perform the task properly. On a busy day, the extra two hours and 40 minutes it takes to train someone else to do the task will probably feel like an inappropriate use of your time. That's human nature. You are likely to think something along these lines: *"Not today! I don't have time to stop what I am doing and spend almost half my day teaching someone else to do something I can do in a few minutes!"*

Let's see. No, let's not just see, let's do the math. Let's say you actually time yourself doing the task and are surprised to discover that from start to finish the task actually takes 27 minutes.

Doing something weekly means it will have to be done 52 times a year. That's 52 times 27 minutes or 1,404 minutes. Now, take 1,404 minutes and divide it by 60 and you get 23 hours and 24 minutes. So, if you go ahead and suck it up and spend the three hours training someone else to do the task today, you will free up 20 hours and 24 minutes over the next year. And if you can find just three more items like that to delegate, you'll free up an extra two weeks next year to focus on more important things.

Now What?

Keep this simple. Find one recurring task a week and apply the math to see if it is a candidate for delegation. Actually time yourself doing it...do not guess. If the task turns out to be a candidate, take the time to teach someone else to do it, and let it go. Keep doing this until you run out of things to delegate. If you run your own small business, don't forget that you can delegate tasks to people who offer virtual assistant services to small businesses.

13
Sometimes Sweat the Small Stuff

What?

Can the flap of a butterfly's wings in Brazil set off a tornado in Texas?

In 1961, Massachusetts Institute of Technology mathematician and meteorologist Edward Lorenz developed a mathematical model to help predict weather. For some reason, he decided to re-examine a previous simulation generated by his computerized model. In order to save time, Lorenz decided not to rerun the entire program. He entered data from his previous printout and restarted the program in the middle rather than at the beginning. Lorenz apparently assumed results of the new simulation would exactly match results of the previous run. The new results weren't even close!

The two calculations quickly began to diverge dramatically and lost any resemblance after just a few "simulation" months. As it turned out, the printout from the previous run rounded numbers to three digits and the internal computer memory rounded to six digits. Therefore, instead of continuing with the previously computed number, in this case .506127, Lorenz restarted the simulation with the rounded number .506. This ever-so-slight variation triggered significant changes in the ultimate outcome of the simulation. Scientists refer to this phenomenon as "sensitive dependence on initial condition."

Years before Lorenz ran his computer program, others referred to this phenomenon as the butterfly effect. The idea that the flapping of a butterfly's wings can create tiny changes in the atmosphere that might cause or prevent major weather patterns somewhere else in the world appeared nine years earlier in a short story by Ray Bradbury about time travel. In 1972, when Lorenz failed to provide a title for a planned presentation on his research to a group of fellow scientists, someone titled his presentation: *Does the Flap of a Butterfly's Wings in Brazil Set Off a Tornado in Texas?*

So What?

Seemingly minor events can make all the difference in the world. Leaders who understand this are in a much better position to create positive, and prevent negative, outcomes for their organization.

Note that the butterfly effect cuts both ways. The flapping of a butterfly's wings in Brazil might trigger changes in the wind and ultimately cause or prevent a tornado from occurring in Texas. The same is true in your organization. Seemingly minor events can *cause* or *prevent* future chaos in an organization. They can also *cause* or *prevent* success.

Now What?

Let's consider a few practical implications of the butterfly effect and what you might do to increase the odds of creating a favorable outcome in your work environment:

Collapse the illusion that the "organization" can get anything done. When we say "the company does this" or "the company does that" what we really mean is that *the individuals who make up the entity* we think of as the company do this or do that. It's a seemingly inconsequential distinction. However, that's the point with the butterfly effect. A small shift in attitude among employees (like a small shift in the wind) can make a huge difference in the ultimate outcome of a group of people working together to accomplish a common cause. When you collapse the illusion that the organization will ever get anything done on its own, you place the full responsibility for getting things done where it belongs...with the individual members of the organization. This, in effect, pulls the rug out from under a lot of future excuses, scapegoat strategies and chaos.

Make sure that goals are clearly defined and responsibilities are clearly understood. This would seem to go without saying. However, for what it is worth, I was handed the results of a survey of 23,000 workers during an ASTD (American Society of Training and Development) meeting a few years ago that indicated only 37 percent of the people surveyed had a clear understanding of what their organization was trying to achieve and why. Everyone in an organization needs to be clear about three things: the goals of the organization, their responsibilities in achieving this outcome, and how their role fits in with their coworkers' roles.

Earlier is Easier. The earlier you pay attention to the flap of a butterfly's wings, the easier it is to deal with and possibly influence the pattern of events that the flap sets in motion. Of course, this applies to the events in the lives of the individuals making up your workgroup. A little easy work on the front-end will prevent huge problems down the road. For example, one big event in the chain of butterfly-effect events that make up the life cycle of an employee is the first day at work on a new job. The first day at work is, in effect, a big "flap" in the person's overall experience with an organization. Regardless of what else happens on that day, make sure any new person on the job understands the big picture of what the organization is trying to achieve and the role of the employees in achieving this outcome. Lack of clarity on the first day of a job is like a flap of the wings in Brazil that ultimately creates a tornado in Texas. Lack of clarity leads directly to low performance and conflict among humans.

Eliminate "us versus them" thinking. A group working together to accomplish a common goal must be clear about their common goal or they will begin to split into subgroups pursuing different versions of the goal (based on their perception or interpretation of the goal). The people in the overall group split into "us versus them" groups and when this starts, it is not unusual for all the groups to begin thinking of the entity referred to as the company, corporation or organization as just another "them" group. Clearly defined goals help prevent "us versus them" thinking.

It would have been nice if you had done all of this on everyone's first day of work. However, I'll bet that didn't always happen. That's OK, the butterfly effect only suggests that sooner is better than later, not that once you miss a flap all opportunity for influence is lost. Do it now! Sit down with your direct reports and clarify:

- *What* your organization is trying to achieve and *why*. Keep it simple. Remember, you can't explain something you do not fully understand. You may need to do a little homework to clarify things in your mind first. That's OK. It will be good for you.

- *Their specific roles* in what your organization is trying to achieve, and *why it is important*.

- *How their roles fit in with their coworkers' roles*.

- That they understand a corporation can only get things done through people who learn to cooperate with each other to attract and retain highly desired *employees*, and to attract and retain highly desired *customers*.

Sit down with your direct reports and go over these issues until you feel everyone clearly understands the big picture. Then ask them to do the same with their direct reports, and so forth and so on down the line. By the way, these sit-down discussions can go both ways. Maybe you are not the boss. Hopefully you feel comfortable going uphill and asking your boss to sit down and go over the same issues and clarify things for you.

When a group works together to improve clarity related to workplace issues, a big "flap" occurs, setting successful things in motion. Look for other butterfly-effect events in your work environment and see what you can do to set things in motion to create a successful outcome in the future.

14
Peace on Earth, Including at Work

What?

Why would a group of people who were literally trying to *kill* each other one day, joyfully *celebrate together* the very next day? And, can you learn any lessons from these people that might help minimize or deal with conflict in your work environment?

On Thursday, December 24, 1914 on the Western Front of the Great War, later known as World War I, opposing troops sat in muddy trenches in the Flanders region of Belgium. Many necessary ingredients for human conflict were present: a miserable physical environment, stress, guns, bullets, and the viewpoint that the opponents were villains, idiots or inhumane barbarians. German soldiers dug into trenches on one side of the battlefield. British, French and Allied soldiers occupied trenches on the other side. In some cases, opposing combatants were less than 100 yards apart and could hear the murmur of each other's voices. The trenches were wet, dirty, cold, crowded and uncomfortable.

It was Christmas Eve and both sides received holiday packages containing food, clothing, tobacco and other items from their respective homelands. Among the items, soldiers on the German side received small Christmas trees and candles. These candles and small trees ultimately triggered a chain of events that within a few hours turned one of the ultimate forms of aggressive behavior – warfare – into cooperation.

As night began to fall, a few German soldiers placed small trees with lighted candles on mounds along the leading edge of their trench. At first, British soldiers shot at the trees. However, the British eventually stopped firing and curiously peered over the edge of their own trench watching as the Germans placed more and more lighted trees on the mounds. Soon after that, the Germans began singing carols. The British didn't understand the words, but they knew the tunes and began singing along with the Germans. Suddenly signs began popping up on the German side saying, "You no fight…We no fight." The British eventually reciprocated by holding up signs that said, "Merry Christmas." As more signs popped up and communication between the two sides escalated, hostility de-escalated. As unlikely as it may seem considering the circumstances, an agreement was reached between the enemy troops. There would be no hostilities for the rest of the night and none Christmas Day. *The opposing sides established an informal Christmas truce!* Soon soldiers from both sides began coming out of their respective trenches into no-man's land. In a short time former enemies were greeting each other and shaking hands; exchanging gifts of wine, tobacco, chocolate, cognac, black bread, biscuits and ham; sharing family photos; dining together; and playing soccer all up and down the battlefield. One British soldier wrote home and reported that the Germans won their particular match by a score of 3-2.

These shared activities temporarily defused the tension and the "us versus them" mentality that fueled the hostilities between the warring troops. Some believe the events that unfolded during those two days in the winter of 1914 almost brought an early end to World War I. In many cases, generals and politicians had to threaten soldiers to get them to reengage in the hostilities. Fighting along certain portions of the front did not resume until after the beginning of the year. After the Christmas Truce, many of the soldiers in the opposing trenches no longer thought of each other as villains, idiots or inhumane barbarians…and they no longer had such a strong desire to kill each other.

The generals and politicians eventually stepped in, transferred troops around, ordered brutal offensive raids and took other actions to restore the "us versus them" mentality among the soldiers. Aggression was rekindled and the war ultimately claimed the lives of nine million soldiers. By some estimates, if you consider civilian casualties (including those due to war-related diseases), more than 70 million people died during the four-year conflict.

So What?

The story of the Christmas Truce is quite thought provoking when you consider the stark contrast in behavior as the level of "us versus them" thinking subsided and was subsequently reintroduced.

Hopefully, you will never have to deal with this level of conflict in your work environment. However, as a high achiever, you should expect some level of conflict, push-back or outright aggression from those who do not share your viewpoint. High achievers break new ground, try new things, do things differently and are masters at overcoming obstacles to success, including uncooperative coworkers.

There is an old saying that states, "Those who say it can't be done should get out of the way of those who are doing it." That's a cute saying, but it's not what happens in a typical organization. Cynics, naysayers and bureaucratic-minded coworkers rarely just get out of the way. If you have participated in the work world for any significant amount of time, I don't have to tell you this. You already understand that no matter how noble your intentions, people are people, and you can usually expect anything from mild to major disagreement from some people no matter what you do or propose.

Now What?

Rather than responding negatively to potential combatants, if and when someone tries to pick a fight with you or create conflict, why not symbolically hold up a sign that says, "I no fight...You no fight"? On second thought, maybe you can literally consider keeping an "I no fight...You no fight" sign handy in your desk drawer. It might prove to be a great tension breaker and conversation starter (and might even provoke some laughter, which is a known tension breaker). Perhaps you can share the story of the Christmas Truce with the person who is disagreeing with you.

In most tense situations between humans, *the first order of business is to do something to resolve or lower the tension*. This is one of the most important lessons related to handling conflict. A tense environment leads directly to poor communication, and you must be able to clearly communicate if you desire to resolve a conflict. Some people make the mistake of getting the cart before the horse, so to speak. They jump into a tense situation with strategies to quickly fix the problem. Their actions often escalate rather than diffuse the tension.

Highly productive people are masters at dealing with and resolving conflicts that might potentially inhibit their long-term success. But how do you get started if you desire to eliminate or minimize conflict in your life?

- *Choose to be the first to initiate action* to eliminate "us versus them" thinking in your work environment, or between you and a coworker. Don't worry that others have not made the same choice yet. Remember, the British shot at the first few Christmas trees that were placed on the edge of the trench. Conflict resolution usually starts when one person decides to try something different. One German soldier was the first to put up a tree. One German soldier was the first to put up a sign. One British soldier was the first to respond with a "Merry Christmas" sign. Be the person who takes the initiative to resolve conflict!

- *Make tension resolution your initial goal* in any conflict situation. Beware of jumping into a conflict situation and escalating the tension. You can buy books and attend courses that specialize in conflict resolution. However, sometimes a single idea is so powerful you can use it as a pattern to provide an underlying fabric for mastery of a skill. Such a powerful idea is imbedded in the Christmas Truce. The main variable in the Christmas Truce story is "us versus them" thinking. In your case, this translates into "me versus you" or "me versus them" thinking. By altering "us versus them" thinking on Christmas Eve in 1914, a handful of soldiers were able to temporarily stop a world war and start a celebration among combatants.

What would you have done if you were a soldier in the trenches on December 24, 1914? More importantly, now that you know a little more about what happens when "us versus them" thinking is present or absent, what do you think you should do about it now? Here's a strategy to consider. Make the following commitment today:

Let there be peace at work and let it begin with me.

15
The Absolute Value of Life Events

What?

Let's explore an old story by an unknown author about feeding wolves:

> One evening an old Cherokee told his grandson about a battle that goes on inside people. He said, "My son, the battle is between two 'wolves' inside us all. One is *evil*. It is anger, envy, jealousy, sorrow, regret, greed, arrogance, self-pity, guilt, resentment, inferiority, lies, false pride, superiority and ego. The other is *good*. It is joy, peace, love, hope, serenity, humility, kindness, benevolence, empathy, generosity, truth, compassion and faith." The grandson thought about it for a minute and then asked his grandfather, "Which one wins?" The old Cherokee simply relied, "The one you feed."

One of the main lessons of this story is that whatever you think about or focus on expands in your life. Think about good things and good things will more likely happen to you. Think about evil or bad things and bad things will more likely happen to you. The old Cherokee gave some pretty clear examples of things that are generally considered good and things that are generally considered evil or bad. However, what if the wolves showing up in your life are neither inherently good nor evil? What about gain, loss, praise, ridicule, credit, blame, joy and suffering? Take a moment to consider these wolves one at a time. What do you think? Are these good wolves or evil wolves?

So What?

First let's tackle the good and evil issue. Most of us are introduced to the concepts of good and evil as very small children. Even before babies can understand words, they can clearly understand facial expressions. For example, they instinctively know from the expression on their mother's face that something is good (approved and desirable) or evil (disapproved and undesirable). As they learn to comprehend words, we bombard them with words that represent the concept of evil such as no, bad, stop, don't do that! *Many children probably grow up believing that the absence of bad is much better than the presence of good.* Maybe that's why so many grown-ups struggle with dysfunctional perfectionism. These people are usually more focused on preventing bad things from happening than pursuing good things. The preference for avoiding bad over pursuing good is reinforced early and often by religious teachers, school teachers and peers who are learning the same things from the same sources for the same reasons. The lessons of good and evil are further reinforced by our own human nature. It just feels natural to quickly classify things as good or bad.

I am not suggesting that good and bad aren't valid concepts in our normal, ordinary, everyday physical world. Thinking of things as good or bad teaches us important things about life that we need to understand to survive when we are not yet intellectually equipped to learn in other ways. However, in a more philosophical or spiritual sense, there is little value in classifying anything as good or bad…and stopping there.

So, since we are philosophical/spiritual beings living in a physical world, we must expand our understanding of these concepts as we learn more about life. The big "So What" of this chapter is that *people who continue to expand their understanding of the absolute value of seemingly good and bad events, significantly increase the probability that they will live a more joyful and productive life.*

Mathematicians use the term "absolute value" to describe the magnitude or numerical value of a number irrespective of whether it is positive or negative. It is a good idea to get better at thinking of the absolute value of people, things and events we encounter, rather than getting too hung up on labeling these encounters as positive or negative.

Now What?

When you encounter an experience in your life you would typically classify as good or bad, ask yourself the following questions, "What is the absolute value of this experience? How might this event be good for me? How might this event be bad for me?" Hopefully these questions will lead to a higher or more accurate truth regardless of how you might initially classify the experience. And the truth, as they say, will set you free!

Let's play around with this way of thinking and explore the eight wolves listed earlier in the chapter.

> **Gain and Loss** – Initially, gain sounds pretty good and loss sounds pretty bad. However, the classification can be easily reversed by simply thinking of these two words

in terms of weight control. But let's explore a more complex matter, money. How many times have you heard about people who experienced significant financial gain and then lost their ability to tell who their true friends were? What about the good news/bad news aspect of winning the lottery? A gain is what it is. And a loss is what it is. They both simply represent potential lessons in life...that's all!

Praise and Ridicule – Praise initially sounds good and ridicule sounds bad. However, we have all heard stories of how excessive praise (for example, fame) caused people to eventually crash and burn, and ridicule drove people to make significant improvements.

Credit and Blame – Both of these experiences have the potential to send us down productive or unproductive paths in life. It's nice to get credit when credit is due, but credit is an external form of determining your value that can lead to problems if you take it too seriously. Getting blamed is no fun, but it can serve as a catalyst for positive changes in your life...or not!

Joy and Suffering – Joy is very pleasant, but it can lead to unhealthy attachment and addiction. And there are entire religions and philosophies based on the idea that suffering creates personal growth and development.

Here is the lesson in all of this. Rather than jump to a good/bad (or good/evil) conclusion, learn to substitute the following three-part process when dealing with patterns of seemingly good or bad experiences:

- Acknowledge the experience.
- Learn from the experience.
- Whether you perceive the experience as good, bad or both, move on at the appropriate time (usually quickly).

We often speak of people who are grounded and centered. They are very good at handling the vicissitudes of life. Such people are probably skilled at properly acknowledging their life experiences, learning from them and quickly moving on. How much more grounded and centered would you be if you used this three-part process when you experienced gain and loss, praise and ridicule, credit and blame, or joy and suffering?

I'm very happy that I encountered the story about the old Cherokee and his grandson. I'm human, so I'll continue to feed wolves from time to time. But I'm also glad I took the time to further explore this story and develop an understanding of how to keep some of the wolves from considering me as a source of food in the first place. In nature, if you cut off the food supply of a species, it eventually becomes extinct. That's probably a pretty good strategy for dealing with our mental wolves. Wolves are neither good nor bad, they are just wolves – teachers, warning signals, guides or gifts! Just like the old Cherokee's story.

16
Busy Behavior: Good or Bad?

What?

Nothing is necessarily wrong, or wrong with you, if you are busy from time to time. Being busy simply means you are fully occupied with an activity or multiple activities. *And that is all it means.* Being busy may or may not equate to being a problem. Of course, it also may or may not equate to being productive.

In order to determine if your busyness, or any behavioral issue, has crossed the line and become a problem, consider four evaluation factors:

> **Frequency** – How often do you deal with this issue?
>
> **Duration** – How long have you been dealing with this issue?
>
> **Intensity** – How much is this issue negatively impacting your productivity?
>
> **Crossover Effect** – Is this issue negatively impacting your ability to live a balanced and joyful life?

If one or more of these factors is noticeably excessive, it's probably a good idea to explore the reasons for your behavior. If all of these factors are excessive, there is a good chance you have a problem.

So What?

Why would an adult feel the need to stay excessively busy? Here are a few possibilities:

- They were raised by parents or caretakers who pushed them to stay extremely busy. Think about it. What kind of words or actions would lead a child to believe that staying busy is a positive attribute and idleness is a negative attribute (as opposed to maintaining a reasonable balance between productive activities and relaxing and restoring their energy)? For example, what were you told about how to spend your weekend days? What kind of guidance did you receive on how to spend your summer days out of school?

- They were raised by parents or caretakers who ceaselessly role-modeled busyness and constantly vocalized the fact that there was never enough time to get everything done. As a child, everything was rush, rush, rush! Therefore, the child constantly got caught up in the vortex of the caretaker's life. For example, consider what some children are learning about how to manage life these days if their parents are digitally connected and available to others 24/7.

- They were pushed to carry a heavy load during their school years. For example, they were strongly advised to take lessons, get involved in sports, join school clubs and organizations, and participate in as many extracurricular activities as possible. All this activity served as a training ground or template for what "successful" adults do to stay on top of things.

- They are driven by "I'm not good enough" or "I don't have enough" beliefs, and think the answer to this dilemma somehow has to do with staying busy.

These are all versions of the same erroneous programming of the psyche. Programming that somehow leads a person to believe that activity equals high value as a human, and inactivity equals low value. This is simply a false economy that makes sense only if you ignore reality. When you are inactive, for whatever reason, are you worth any less as a human being? Is someone who maintains an appropriate balance between activity and inactivity worth less as a human than a workaholic? Taking things to an extreme, is a loved one in a coma worth any less to you because they are not busy? For a moment, forget about the fact that the human spirit of one individual is always equal in value to the human spirit of any other individual. In the end, excessive activity isn't even a very good strategy for generating material wealth. Centered, grounded, well-balanced people have just as much (or more) potential to generate abundant incomes and wealth over their lifetimes as excessively busy people. And it is likely that the former will enjoy their tangible rewards significantly more than the latter.

Equating busyness to value as a human, or connecting it in some way to the creation of a productive life, is common these days. It is highly understandable based on some people's upbringing. But it is based on false beliefs. It is an illusion.

Now What?

The logic of the busyness illusion falls apart on its own when you become aware that it is, in fact, an illusion. If you frequently say or think that you do not have time to get everything done, if you feel the activity level in your life is too intense, or if other areas of your life (marriage, personal relationships with family and friends, health, etc.) are suffering because you are unable to devote time and energy to them, it is time to do something about it. It is time to see if you can determine the source of your crusade to fill your day with activity. Ironically, you can only do this if you are willing to give up your busyness and take time to think and reflect on the source of your behavior. Here's something for you to think about:

Be still and know that it is OK.

For those of you who are ready, this is an eight-word formula for successfully dispelling the busyness illusion. This is a statement of reality. And illusions cannot survive in the presence of awareness and reality. If you sense that your busyness is becoming or has become a problem, try this: Be still and know that it is OK. Doing this may not be easy for someone whose nervous system is used to busyness. So just start by trying it for a few minutes. Then decide how much stillness you need in your life to balance out the busyness…and decide it is OK. Either way, your value as a human will remain the same, and that's the most important point.

17
The Power of Adaptability

What?

It's good to be smart and adaptable. If not, you have to take what life gives you. If you are a peppered moth, this may mean becoming a snack for a hungry bird. Here's the highly summarized story of the perilous plight of the peppered moth. The facts:

- Some peppered moths are predominantly light colored.
- Some peppered moths are predominantly dark colored.
- Some trees (where peppered moths hang out) are predominantly light colored.
- Some trees (where peppered moths hang out) are predominantly dark colored.
- Birds think peppered moths are tasty and like to eat them.
- Birds are most likely to eat the peppered moths they can easily see.

So what's a peppered moth to do? Or more importantly, where should a weary peppered moth land and hang out for a few minutes of rest? You can mentally run through the possibilities and finish the story.

They say a picture is worth a thousand words. Put the words "peppered moth" in your Internet search engine and select the "Images" search function. You will quickly see why peppered moths that have adapted to the color of their environment are more likely to survive and prosper.

The bottom line is it's very beneficial to be able to adapt to your environment or select an environment that improves your chances of survival and success.

So What?

So what can we learn from peppered moths that can help us improve our chances of career survival and success? Let's use the facts related to the plight of the peppered moth as a template and apply them to humans. Here's just one example of how the story might unfold:

- Some people are predominantly extroverted and spontaneous.

- Some people are predominantly introverted and methodical.

- Some careers call for people to be predominantly extroverted and spontaneous (for example, some people-oriented careers where you must constantly interact with others and operate in a highly unstructured environment).

- Some careers call for people to be predominantly introverted and methodical (for example, some task-oriented careers where you must work alone in a highly structured environment).

- Bosses like downsizing during tough economic times and especially like to get rid of people who do not seem to be a good fit for their job.

Once again, I think you can finish the story.

Now What?

Let's draw a few conclusions:

- Moths are not smart enough to know they should adapt to their environment or select a beneficial environment. They don't really understand the implications of landing on a dark versus light tree.

- Some people are like moths. They land a job that calls for them to be extroverted when they are introverted, or spontaneous when they are methodical. Or, vice versa. Or, they mismatch some other predominant personality trait.

- Other people understand the implications of personality-trait mismatches. They take the time to fully explore and understand their predominant personality traits and then...*they wisely select an environment and career path (or make changes to their current career path) that will most likely allow them to take advantage of their strengths and minimize their struggles.*

If you haven't already done so, consider having your personality assessed. Supposedly, there are more than 200 personality assessment tools on the market. Many of these are available online for a minimal investment. Most people who deal with the assessment process have their favorite or favorites. Check it out for yourself and pick the one you like. Or, if you have trouble deciding or finding an assessment tool you like, visit www.dmetraining.com and take a look at the information on the assessment tool I prefer, and why. Once you complete an assessment, study the results and look carefully for matches and mismatches between your dominant personality traits and what you are called to do on an ongoing basis at work.

Does your job energize or drain you? Matches tend to energize you and mismatches tend to drain you. In terms of your career choice, are you a dark-colored moth on a light-colored tree, or vice versa? In the end, take full responsibility for the design of your career path. In other words, know thyself, and as Willie S. said, "To thine own self be true."

18
Remember to Create New Memories

What?

Several years ago I read that the current shelf life of a Ph.D.'s formal education was only about 18 months. Can you believe that? Even highly educated people must keep upgrading their knowledge base or they will be obsolete in a year or two. As knowledge continues to expand, you can expect the shelf life of your formal education and training to diminish even faster. So how do you go about upgrading your knowledge base and keeping up with the times? Simply remember to *create new, high-quality memories* every day related to your chosen profession.

There is an old saying, "What's in the well comes up in the bucket!" When you encounter challenging situations in life, it is good to have a "well" full of high-quality memories to draw from in order to size up the situation and respond appropriately. Understanding a little more about how knowledge gets into your "brain-well" might help explain why it is important to choose ongoing and lifelong learning as one of your highest priorities.

So What?

Neuroscientists usually talk about the fact that we see, hear, smell, taste and experience touch, pain and temperature with our *brain,* not our eyes, ears, nose, tongue and skin. What exactly do they mean by this? They are talking about the fascinating process of getting information from our external world into our internal world through sensory input processing. *All sensory experiences are ultimately created inside the brain.* Scientists also estimate that eyesight provides the brain with more information than all other senses combined. So let's use eyesight to illustrate how we take in and process information.

Most of us think we "see" with our eyes. If you haven't explored the details of eyesight, you may believe that your eyes essentially take mental photos of objects in the environment and somehow send the "developed photos" to your brain intact. That's not the way the process works.

With apologies to vision experts, here is a highly oversimplified version of how the process of vision works. Light waves, bouncing off objects in the external world, enter our eyes and ultimately make it to the back of our eyeballs to a place called the retina. Specialized cells in the retina convert the light waves into the primary language of the nervous system, electrochemical impulses. Then an electrochemical relay process takes over and sends information through the optic nerve and on various pathways in the brain. In the case of eyesight, the converted electrical impulses are routed to more than 30 areas of the brain (or hundreds, in the opinion of some neuroscientists) for further processing. For example, separate areas of the brain determine what you are seeing, other areas determine where the object you are seeing is located in space, other areas determine the shape, color, etc. of the object. Ultimately all the pieces of the neural puzzle are merged and an image of what we "see" is reconstructed inside our brain. Whew! And that was the highly oversimplified version!

Although vision was used as the example, all the conventional forms of sensory input are processed in a similar way. Light waves, sound waves, molecules floating through the air, molecules we ingest and pressure from physical contact all go through this process. Everything we see, hear, smell, taste and physically feel is converted to electrical impulses and routed through the brain for processing and reconstruction. So how does the brain *give meaning* to the things we encounter in our environment?

Most of the work of interpreting meaning is processed by a part of our brain called the temporal lobe. Among other functions, the temporal lobe is central to the process we call memory. That's ultimately where all this talk about what goes on inside the brain was headed. *We typically comprehend things we encounter in our environment by comparing or associating them in some way with things we already understand.* In our case, the database of "things we already understand" is called our memory. Sensory processing relies heavily on our memories when interpreting and reconstructing images inside our brain.

Why is understanding this sensory process important? The only language the nervous system understands is electrical and chemical. So in order to learn anything new, you must constantly stir up these electrochemical processes that kick-start and sustain the learning process. And if all these electrochemical impulses must be reconstructed inside our brain when we process incoming information, it clearly shows how much room for error exists if we don't possess a *high quantity* of *high-quality* memory files.

People with good memory files are better at accurately perceiving reality. *Among a group of people, the most successful person is usually the one whose viewpoint of reality is most closely related to reality.* For example, there was a time in history when almost everyone thought the world was flat. How limiting do you suppose this belief was for a seafaring explorer during that era? How much fear and anxiety do you suppose this faulty memory file generated among sailors? There was a time when most doctors had no memory files related to germs. They didn't believe in germs mainly because they couldn't see them, and didn't even bother to wash their hands before surgery. Then someone invented the microscope. Almost overnight, the memory files of doctors all over the world were upgraded. Countless lives were, and continue to be, saved by this particular memory upgrade.

Now What?

As we get involved in the day-to-day activities of our careers, we sometimes forget to place a high priority on the process of constantly upgrading our memory files related to our chosen profession. Highly successful people constantly do three things:

- Increase the *quantity* of their memory files.
- Upgrade the *quality* of their memory files.
- Upgrade the *connections* or *associations* between and among their memory files.

Here's a plan to keep you on track and up-to-date:

- Every profession, career, job or whatever you want to call it has a few areas of knowledge considered the "basics." In the game of baseball, hitting, running, catching and throwing are the basics. Determine the basics of your chosen profession. For example, if you are in sales you might designate prospecting, presentations, handling objections, closing and post-sale follow up as the basics. Don't worry about getting the undisputedly right answer to this question. You can always add a basic as your knowledge increases.

- Increase the quantity and quality of your memory files related to each of the basics by learning one new thing every day or increasing your depth of knowledge in some way (read an article, read a book, talk to an expert, try something new, etc.).
- Take time every day to slow down for a few moments, challenge the quality of your existing memory files, and think about how all these pieces fit together.

Neuroscientists now know that much of the memory consolidation process occurs during sleep. Consolidation is their fancy word for moving something from temporary memory to more permanent memory. Scientists who study sleep also use another term called hypnagogic. The hypnagogic state is the state between being awake and falling asleep. You've laid your head on the pillow, you are getting groggy, but you are not quite yet asleep. Every day, pick a "new memory" related to your basics. Play around with it all day, think about it, read up on it, write notes about it on index cards and look at the cards throughout the day, talk to people about it, try to find something wrong with it, try to prove something right about it, determine what you have to accept on faith for now about it, etc. Then summarize your memory for the day and think about it when you are in the hypnagogic state. Let sleep take it from there.

If you're not ready to define the basics of your profession, why not read a chapter of this book right before bedtime each night for the next few weeks and sleep on it. Whatever you decide to do, have a hypnagogic happening tonight!

19
A Few Elements of Change

What?

In 1819 the first section of the Erie Canal connecting the Great Lakes with the Atlantic Ocean was completed. The entire canal was opened six years later on October 26, 1825. Here's an excerpt of a letter that Martin Van Buren, later the governor of New York, supposedly wrote to the president of the United States expressing his views on the canal and the threat of the expanding railroad system:

> *The canal system of this country is being threatened by the spread of a new form of transportation known as "railroads." As you may well know, railroad carriages are pulled at the enormous speed of 15 mph by engines, which, in addition to endangering life and limb of passengers, roar and snort their way through the countryside. The Almighty certainly never intended that people should travel at such breakneck speed.*

There is some speculation that Van Buren didn't really write this. It's a bit hard to believe that he did since it wouldn't be a very smart thing for a public figure to say, much less put in writing. Of course, Van Buren was a politician very involved with the approval and funding of the Erie Canal, so it makes some sense, if you consider the political and financial ramifications of the emergence of the railroad. However, even if he didn't write it, if you study the history of that era and explore the attitudes of people during the early 1800s, Van Buren's letter is representative of the way many people felt about the emergence of the "evil" railroads. They strongly opposed this symbol of change.

People who financed and controlled the railroads got caught in the same trap later in history as new forms of transportation developed. Were these people who were running major industries and our country bad, stupid, stubborn or foolish? No, they were just normal people acting as you might expect them to act. They were humans! And although humans are good at many things, *neither nature nor nurture encourages humans to embrace change.*

So What?

Nurture encourages us to adopt comfort-zone positions in life. This is why many people choose the same religion, political party, attitudes and preferences as their parents or caretakers. However, for now, let's focus on how nature opposes change.

Americans spend an estimated $30 billion a year on diet programs and products. That's a lot of money that overweight people give to other people just to help them change their eating habits! That's so much money that if you started right now and put a hundred bucks a second through a shredder, 24 hours a day, it would take you almost 10 sleepless years to go through $30 billion. And the kicker is that most of the $30 billion is totally wasted. Most diets are doomed from the start for the following reasons:

- Human behavior is controlled by different but overlapping parts of the brain and nervous system. These overlapping brain structures try to play together nicely if possible, but it is not unusual for them to fight like siblings. It's sort of like a fight between a two-year-old and his five-year-old brother. In a contest for control of behavior, the more powerful and primitive older parts of the brain and nervous system pretty much "kick butt" when they are fighting the younger, less powerful parts.

- Think about it. The most common response to the desire to lose weight is to lower your intake of food. So most dieters think of *all* the weight they want to lose and decide, "Starting tomorrow, I'm going to take care of this problem once and for all. I'm going on a crash diet…goodbye feast, hello famine!"

- Eat less food. What a brilliant idea! The younger components of your brain and nervous system, in charge of logic, reasoning, planning and controlling impulsive behavior, immediately "get it" and, in effect, say, "Hey, this is a great idea. I'm all for it! Let's stop this counterproductive behavior that is causing this human to eat so much food." These nervous system components tell the rest of the body to "implement the new behavior strategy." The order is given and the body begins to execute the command. Let the behavior change begin!

- Meanwhile, after a relatively short time, older internal brain structures lurking in the lower regions of the brain "wake up" the more primitive components of the nervous system. These primitive "neural watchdogs" raise their heads, scratch behind their left ear, look around and say, "What's going on here? Uh oh, this human is starving! OK, here's what we're going to do. Release some of that stuff into the bloodstream that will make them eat like a joint-smoking wolf at midnight! If you

> have to, use that binge-inducing hormone we used last time this happened. And shut down that system that makes them feel satisfied after they eat for a few minutes. I want lots of food shoved down this guy's alimentary canal and I want it there in a hurry! I can't go back to sleep until this is taken care of, so get on it right now!"

The bottom line is if you try to change too much, too soon, you will rarely accomplish your goal. Your plan is doomed from the start. One simple way to avoid this and increase the odds that your desired change will survive is to simply start small and avoid waking up the neural watchdogs. In this example, don't try to lose so much body weight in such a short time. Shoot for a 5 percent to 10 percent loss, give your body systems time to get comfortable with your new weight level, and then go for another 5 percent to 10 percent.

I used weight loss as an example. However, you can substitute other changes (eliminating excessive multitasking, procrastination, workaholism, excessive e-mailing, etc.), and substitute other neural watchdogs, and the lessons you learn from this example pretty much remain the same. It all has to do with the physiology of change and something called homeostasis. That's why it's a good idea to understand a little more about the physiology of change.

Now What?

Understanding the physiology of change helps you change.

Humans are designed by nature to resist change. Homeostasis, a general process that describes this resistance to change, likes to keep things just as they are. If your body temperature, heartbeat, blood flow and other vital functions of your anatomy vary even slightly, various components of your nervous system snap into action and try to restore order as soon as possible. Your body, of course, views restoring order as getting back to whatever it is used to experiencing. The powerful, older and controlling elements of the brain and nervous system issue orders to the rest of your body systems to "get things back to normal." There are at least two natural processes that have the potential to override homeostasis and facilitate a desired change: repetition and strong emotional influences. Therefore if you are really serious about implementing a change, do one of two things:

1. Identify the behavior that goes along with the change (the behavior that represents the change or will produce it) and repeat the behavior over, and over for at least 21 days. If the new behavior doesn't feel totally natural after doing this, repeat it for another 21 days. Some advisors like to throw around 21 days as the magic timeframe for change. It may take more time than this or it may take less. Different changes require different time periods, and different people have different timeframes for change. It also helps if you attach the new habit you are trying to establish to an already well-established habit. For most people, this might mean putting a sticky note reminding you of your new habit on the mirror where you shave, put on your makeup, brush your teeth, etc.

2. Attach the strongest emotional reason you can think of to the desired change. Emotions fall into six broad categories: joy, sadness, anger, surprise, disgust and fear.

Any of the emotions will help you get the job done, but if you have a choice, why not choose joy? Whenever possible, focus on the gain rather than the give-up! Habits are driven by your memory. In the case of repetition, you encode memory (and reroute or alter neural pathways) by doing something over and over. That works, but a much faster and effective way of burning something into your memory is attaching strong emotions to it. That's why you have such a good memory of some of the peak emotional experiences (good and bad) in your life. Back to the diet example, when you grab a snack that might be considered junk-food, stop. As you hold it in your hand, think of a pleasant emotion related to your goal, like your clothes fitting better or something else that really feels good to you related to being healthier. Put the snack back and enjoy the gain (or lack of weight gain in this case) aspect of your behavior and don't focus on the give-up.

Counter hopelessness with hope.

If all else fails and you get to the point of feeling hopeless, seek an external source of hope. In the book *Change or Die* by Alan Deutschman, you can learn about some specific techniques used to help hopeless people find new hope and ultimately make life-altering changes. For example, Deutschman discusses several studies that attempted to determine the best form of psychotherapy. In the end, the studies reveal that all forms of therapy worked equally as well. The form of therapy didn't matter as much as the relationship with the therapist. In many cases, it seems that *the decision to go to a therapist somehow inspires a new sense of hope among previously hopeless people.*

As a practical matter, if you've unsuccessfully launched a strategy for change several times, maybe you shouldn't keep trying the same thing or wait until you feel hopeless. Find someone who is an expert at facilitating the kind of change you desire and ask them, pay them, do whatever it takes to get them to help you. It's a real sign of strength to recognize that you need help and ask for it.

These are just a few basic elements of change. Change is too big a topic for one chapter in one book. I have given you a few ideas on how to better understand and implement changes. My ultimate suggestion is to make the study of how humans change, and why they don't change, an ongoing topic for exploration. Although you will rarely – maybe never – find a high school, college or graduate course on the elements of change, it is one of the most important issues in life. When you begin to focus on this topic, the appropriate resources will magically appear in your life. Books such as *Change or Die* by Deutschman, or *Following Through* by Steve Levinson and Pete Greider, and others will magically show up. People who can help you will show up. Who knows, if you really need to learn how quickly and permanently strong emotions can create change in your life, Jane Elliott's video titled *A Class Divided* may show up.

Understanding more about the basic elements of change is a productive use of your time. Give it a try!

20
Exploring the Source of Unproductive Behavior

What?

The year was 1933. The place was an operating room at McGill University Hospital in Montreal. Dr. Wilder Penfield, a brain surgeon, accidentally stumbled across something that was simply difficult to believe.

Dr. Penfield developed a technique, referred to as the Montreal Procedure, helping pinpoint the area of the brain causing his patients' epileptic seizures. This newly developed surgical procedure was performed on patients who remained fully conscious during their operations. He opened a large section of their skull *while they were fully alert and conscious*. By doing this, he was able to communicate with them as he used his electronic probe to map out the functions of various parts of their brains. For example, he might touch his probe to a certain area of the brain and the patient would comment on a tingling sensation in his nose. Or he might touch the probe to another area of the brain and the patient's little finger would twitch. On this particular day in 1933, as he touched his electronic probe to the temporal lobe of a middle-aged woman, she suddenly said, "I seem to see myself as I was when I was having my baby."

The temporal lobe, which is now closely associated with the functioning of long-term memory, was still unknown territory to medical professionals. Penfield made a note of this strange occurrence and continued with the operation. However, during the next 20 years many of his patients experienced the same flashback experiences during similar operations. The patients described the experiences as more than just recalling or remembering long-forgotten events. It seemed as if they "relived all that they had been aware of in the earlier period of time as if in a moving-picture flashback." Penfield's probe was somehow triggering the instant retrieval of previously forgotten events as well as the *feelings* associated with the events. It was as if the patients had traveled back in time and were in the middle of actually experiencing the past events in the current moment.

So What?

Many people who learned about Dr. Penfield's probing experience drew the following conclusions:

- Everything that has ever happened to us is stored somewhere in our brains. Therefore, under the right circumstances, we can recall anything that has happened to us from birth (and some think prior to birth). The *feelings* associated with these events may be driving our current behavior, even if we can't recall the *facts* associated with the events.

- Perhaps not every single event has been stored in our long-term memory. However, many of the significant personality-shaping events are stored somewhere in our brain, psyche, cellular memory or nervous system, and can be recalled under certain circumstances. These events and feelings from the past can somehow be triggered and drive our current behavior.

- We can better understand our current behavior if we learn to track it to these past events that somehow still strongly influence our choices of how to respond to current events in our lives.

Since I am always interested in anything that might influence human productivity, I was intrigued by the possible implications of Penfield's findings. Things that happened to us in the past can, and often do, strongly influence our current choices in life. For example, here are some examples of how childhood messages may affect current behavior:

- "Look both ways before crossing the street." This message served us well as children and is still serving us well as adults.

- "Republicans are bad and Democrats are good." This message may cause us to ignore the facts and consistently vote for Democrats. It may also cause us to interpret "facts" in a way that favors the Democratic Party and platform.

- "Democrats are bad and Republicans are good." This message may cause us to ignore the facts and consistently vote for Republicans. It may also cause us to interpret "facts" in a way that favors the Republican Party and platform.

- "Always buy this brand of car, gas, insurance, clothes, etc." In my case, because of my dad's unpleasant experience with a certain brand of tires (and the fact that his negative comments were overheard by his then very young son), I would have a hard time forcing myself to buy that particular brand to this day. I don't even know the details of the disagreement. I just know I wouldn't feel good about buying that brand of tires.

- "Don't talk to strangers." This is another message that served us well as children. However, what if you are now an adult working as a salesperson? Combine this message with the old standards, "It's not polite to stick your nose in other people's business," or "Children are to be seen and not heard," and you have a salesperson who will be uncomfortable prospecting and asking qualifying questions. In short, you will have a salesperson who is hesitant to sell.

Take a moment to think about your childhood messages. How much old, obsolete or incorrect stuff is still in there influencing your behavior? Some of your current self-defeating, clutter-causing, non-productive behavior may be triggered by things that occurred in the past.

Some people refer to these messages as tapes. When memories are somehow activated, it's as if a tape or movie is playing inside your head. So if these tapes exist, how do we retrieve the old memories? It is easier than you think. When we exchange words, voice tone and body language with each other, we are often triggering each other's long-term memories.

For example, if you hear the word dog it will cause your brain to retrieve an image of a dog. For some of you it will be a large dog. Some of you will visualize a small dog. Some will picture a white dog, some a black dog. For some of you, the word dog will trigger emotions related to a frightening encounter with a neighborhood dog when you were a child, or it will retrieve pleasant emotions related to an existing or previous pet. If you hear the words *The Godfather* or *Schindler's List* it may cause your brain to retrieve memories and emotions related to an entire movie. In a similar way, day-to-day events cause your brain to retrieve memories and emotions that may help explain your current behavior.

Certain words, voice tones and facial expressions can make us feel happy. Others can make us feel sad, angry or afraid. In the case of words, your sense of sight (reading words) or hearing can conjure up forgotten memories of events, feelings about them, or both. All five senses serve as memory triggers all day long, every day of our lives. Therefore, *sight, sound, taste, touch and smell perform the same function as Dr. Penfield's probe.*

Now What?

One of the keys to understanding behavior is recognizing what serves as our Penfield probe as we live our daily lives. Many of our behavior-shaping experiences occurred in the first few years of our lives. Memories of some of those events may be driving behavior that is currently serving you well, and other memories may be driving behavior that is not serving you well. Retrieving past memories can provide you with fascinating clues to help explain, and possibly modify, current behavior.

Think about these questions (substitute "main caregiver" instead of father or mother when appropriate):

- What were your father's main life-messages to you?
- What were your mother's main life-messages to you?
- What were your siblings' main messages to you?
- What were your early teachers' main messages to you?

These are significant questions! Answering these questions and others like them can reveal a lot about your current behavior. It is likely that you either went along with these messages or you rebelled against them and made a choice to do the opposite when you became an adult. If your parents are still living, ask them about the messages (tapes) they received from their parents (your grandparents). You will likely discover some interesting things that will help you understand their parenting techniques and some of your current behavior. Asking these questions might help you discover some of your primary emotional triggers.

As you ponder your responses to these questions, think of how these messages may be driving your current behavior. What kind of feelings do these questions trigger? Many of you may find that these questions trigger memories that explain some of your self-defeating behavior including:

- Always being in a hurry or rushed
- Constantly fighting clutter
- Overcommitting and overpromising
- Procrastinating
- Not being able to stay focused on important tasks
- Not being able to get closure on important issues

You do not have to always understand the source of a problem to solve it...but it helps. Play around with this idea and see if you can discover any tapes that might be worth exploring. Pay close attention to the Penfield probe-like events in your typical day that activate various forms of self-defeating behavior. Does that look from your boss that triggers anxiety look somewhat like the looks your dad or mom used to give you when they were disappointed with your behavior? Does someone's voice tone remind you of being scolded as a child? Do certain phrases, such as "you ought to" or "you should" make you feel angry, rebellious or depressed? Do certain sights, sounds or smells trigger strong emotions? What are some of your strong emotional triggers? Think about it!

21
The History of Jane's Perfectionism

What?

Jane Flawless made all As in the first, second, third and fourth grades. At Jane's school, students who made straight As were given fancy blue ribbons to take home with their report cards. Every grading period Jane and her parents conducted a little ritual to celebrate her good grades. They would take the report card out of the envelope and look at it in great detail (even though they knew what the grades were going to be before they opened it), and then take out the blue ribbon and put it on the bulletin board in Jane's room. Since there were four grading periods each year, all the ribbons for all the years were lined up straight-and-true on Jane's bulletin board in rows of four. At this point she had 17 ribbons on her bulletin board because, as expected, she made straight As for the first grading period of the fifth grade.

During the second grading period of the fifth grade, Jane made her first B. She was disappointed. She felt she had tried just as hard as usual during that grading period. However, she had trouble with one test, in one subject, on one day, and it pulled her grade down to a B. Things weren't so bad. When you made a B you still got a ribbon. As a matter of fact, you got the same kind of ribbon except for the color. Because of her one B, she got a red ribbon instead of a blue one. That evening, when Jane's parents took her report card out of the envelope and looked at it they were shocked. It was as if they only saw one thing on the report card...the B. Jane's dad took the red ribbon out of the envelope, looked at it disgustingly, and said, "Young lady, come with me!" Although Jane's dad worked in his downtown office most of the time, he also maintained an office at home. Jane, her mom, and her dad went into her dad's office. Then her dad put the red ribbon through his paper shredder, turned to Jane and said, "We have no use for this color ribbon in this house!" Jane didn't quite know what to think about her dad's comment. "Yes sir," she said, and went to her room and stared at her bulletin board.

Fortunately, Jane got back on track and made straight As for the rest of the year. Unfortunately, there was an empty space in row five of her bulletin board. Not noticing the empty space was impossible. Every time she saw it, the sight of the empty space triggered memories of her dad's office, his disappointment and the shredder. She ultimately decided it was silly to put ribbons on her bulletin board and took them all down.

Jane made excellent grades throughout the rest of her academic career. She was valedictorian of her graduating class in both high school and college. Because of her excellent academic performance, she was highly sought after by the most desirable employers in her field of expertise. Jane was a results-oriented, no-nonsense person, so she accepted an offer from a results-oriented, no-nonsense firm. Because she was so decisive and held herself to the highest possible standards, she was quickly promoted to a senior management position. She took over for another highly successful manager who was promoted to the next level. Four other managers reported directly to her and more than 100 people worked in her department. The department she now managed was known as a stepping stone for high achievers. It was the "New York, New York" of departments. If you could make it there, you could make it anywhere in the firm! At this point, it looked as if the sky was the limit for Jane.

In less than six months, Jane's world crumbled. Her department was in chaos. The departmental bottom line had plummeted. Workplace warfare had broken out! The four managers who reported directly to Jane were literally at war with each other. Morale among all the employees had tanked. Employee turnover was skyrocketing. To make matters worse, the most talented staff people were leaving and only the mediocre people stayed. Jane's boss fired her! When Jane asked why she was being fired, her boss said, "Jane, we've already been over this many times. Your inability to let go and delegate responsibility to your subordinates has created utter chaos in your department. Your quickness to criticize others has spread virally throughout the department and the level of hostility is simply intolerable."

So What?

Jane's story illustrates the potential long-term cost of making the price of a mistake too high. In Jane's case, the seeds of dysfunctional perfectionism were planted in the fifth grade, nurtured throughout her remaining educational career, and came into full bloom in later years. At this point, unless someone intervenes and helps Jane understand that making mistakes is a normal part of a well-lived life, she is doomed to repeat her performance as an over-critical boss unable to effectively delegate and run a successful department...if she gets another chance. Jane is simply acting out what she learned from her parents, who probably meant well and were simply trying to help Jane excel in life.

Now What?

You will inevitably run into a lot of "Janes" during your career (of course, you might just as likely run into a male version of Jane). Your boss may be a Jane, your coworkers may be Janes, you may serve on a committee with a Jane, your clients may be Janes and *you* may be a Jane. So, what do you do if you encounter one of these people in your work environment? What do you do if you are one of these people?

The normal response to a hyper-critical, controlling perfectionist is probably frustration or anger. However, you can deal more effectively with a perfectionist if you try understanding and compassion. These people, although they are usually the last to know it, need help. I told you the story of Jane's earlier life to help you understand that Jane, and people like her, are not necessarily bad or evil people. More often than not, they are just doing what they were taught to do by people they respected.

Here are some things you might consider if you encounter a Jane in your work environment:

- First of all, don't take the things that Jane does personally! Remember, she is acting out a pattern that was established long before you came on the scene. If you think you need help learning to do this, read and reread *The Four Agreements* by don Miguel Ruiz, and pay very close attention to the second agreement which states: Don't Take Anything Personally. I know this is easier said than done. However, highly productive people do not spend much time getting caught up in other people's dramas. This is a good life lesson to learn whether you encounter a Jane or not.

- Understand that Jane's behavior is probably driven by the fear of making some sort of mistake. Find out more about her specific fear, the mistake she is trying to avoid, and gain her trust related to this issue. Think about what you can do to reduce Jane's fears.

- Do not allow yourself to shift into victim mode. If you become a victim, you relinquish any power or leverage you may have to solve the problem. Think of Jane as a teacher rather than a persecutor. What are you supposed to be learning as a result of her actions and this experience? What will you do differently if you encounter such a person in the future (as you inevitably will)?

- Remember, you always have the option of moving on and getting out of a toxic work environment. Sometimes life is too short to tolerate certain things.

And what if you are a Jane? If so, begin thinking of your daily life as an ongoing series of three-part events. First, something *triggers a thought* and stimulates the parts of your brain responsible for interpreting the events in your life. Second, you *interpret the event* by comparing it to your memories and personal beliefs, which may or may not be accurate, logical or rational. Your general choices are to interpret the event as a positive event, a negative event or a neutral event. Third, you *respond to the event*, typically with one of the big-six forms of behavior: joy, sadness, anger, surprise, disgust or fear.

As you grow older and establish habitual response patterns, it is easy to lose sight of the fact that the second step – interpretation – is occurring. Over time, we all develop comfort-zone interpretations and responses which drive our comfort-zone behavior.

For example, Jane is probably unaware that the ribbon-shredding experience in the fifth grade has any connection to her current inability to delegate or her tendency to be overly critical. Jane's behavior feels right to her because she was taught from a young age to avoid mistakes at all cost. Jane needs to somehow come to the realization that her belief system related to making mistakes needs updating. She needs to understand that it is time to let go of her childhood understanding of how the world works, and develop more mature beliefs about what it means to be human. Jane needs to understand that the *pursuit of excellence,* including learning from mistakes, is a healthy human activity. The relentless pursuit of perfection, that includes intolerance for mistakes, is not.

22
The History of John's Indecision

What?

When Johnny Pawn was very little, his parents made decisions for him. Since Johnny was just a baby at the time, it was good that his parents made decisions for him. They were good-hearted, responsible, caring people and only wanted the best for him. Then the day came when Johnny decided he wanted to make some of his own decisions. He was still very little, but that was OK because the decisions he wanted to make were very simple. He felt he could easily handle them on his own. However, his parents decided it would be best if they kept making even very simple decisions for Johnny. For example, one day he decided he was not finished playing with his little toy car and was not ready to put it away. He wasn't paying much attention to the toy car at the time, but his intention was to get back to it in a minute. His parents felt otherwise, and decided it was time to put the toy car away. Johnny was still too young to talk, so he couldn't explain in words to his parents that he would rather leave the toy out where he could see it and play with it when he felt like it. After repeated attempts to get his parents to understand his decision, he gave up and accepted the fact that it must be time to quit paying attention to his toy car and put it away.

Events similar to this happened more often as he got older and learned more and more about how the world works. Johnny was smart and very good at recognizing patterns. He quickly noticed that if he accepted his parents' decisions sooner rather than later, it pleased them immensely. He liked the feeling he experienced when he pleased his parents. He also realized that his parents were very important people. After all, they gave him food, kept him warm and protected him in many ways. It was best just to go along with them. He decided that, in general, it was probably best to go along with everyone. This decision and this strategy seemed to work well for him as he grew older. During his teens he felt frustrated at times that he didn't get to do what he wanted to do if it conflicted with what his parents wanted him to do, but they were taking even better care of him now. They bought him a car and pretty much anything else he wanted. Overall, his strategy worked well for him except for the occasional feelings of frustration.

As John got older, he got better at pleasing people, especially his teachers and professors in high school and college. He was a very good student and made excellent grades. Because of his stellar academic performance in college, he got a great job offer when he graduated from college, and went to work for a top firm in his chosen field of expertise. His new employer had an excellent career development program. For the next few years, John knew exactly what he needed to do to be successful, because important issues were communicated clearly during his career development training. Nothing about the training program was difficult for John. He was quickly labeled a fast-tracker. Basically, all he had to do was "keep his nose clean" and please the people who made promotion decisions, and he was on his way to the top. After completing the career development program faster than anyone had ever completed it, John was made manager of his own department. He took over for another highly successful manager who was promoted to the next level. Four other managers now reported directly to John and more than 100 people worked in his department. This particular department was known to be a stepping stone for high performers. It was the "New York, New York" of departments. If you could make it there, you could make it anywhere in the firm!

So What?

In less than six months, John's world crumbled. His department was in chaos. The departmental bottom line had plummeted. Workplace warfare had broken out! The four managers who reported directly to John were literally at war with each other. Morale among all the employees had tanked. Employee turnover was skyrocketing. To make matters worse, the most talented people were leaving and only the mediocre people stayed. John's boss fired him! When John asked why he was being fired, his boss said, "John, we've already been over this many times. Your inability to make a decision has created utter chaos in your department."

Now What?

Does this story sound a bit familiar? John Pawn and Jane Flawless (from the previous chapter) ended up in the same place for different reasons…or did they? In one sense, they failed for the same reason. They both failed to escape the gravitational pull of their childhood experiences.

Most children (and young adults) spend the first 18 to 20-something years of their lives trying to figure out and comply with what others (parents, teachers, preachers, coaches, etc.) want them to do. This is a necessary part of their development. It is normal for young people to look to others for help in figuring out how the world works. Unfortunately, the people offering guidance do not always understand exactly how the world works. For example, if you were raised by parents with a fear-based, scarcity, non-trusting mentality, there is a good chance you developed a similar mentality. If you were raised by one or more alcoholic caregivers or abusive parents, there is a good chance you picked up some, shall we say, less than accurate beliefs about how the world works. There is little value in playing the blame game with your parents if you truly want to resolve any of these issues. They were probably just passing on what they learned from their childhood caregivers.

So what does all this mean to you today? If you haven't already done so, it's a good idea to take an inventory of your beliefs and make sure they are really *your* beliefs. It's time to upgrade your beliefs and core values. As you can see from the stories about Jane Flawless and John Pawn, not escaping some of your childhood influences can place serious limitations on your potential to joyfully and productively participate in life. Here are a few areas to think about:

- What is the best response to mistakes?
- Am I making my own life decisions or am I really just complying with someone else's agenda?
- What did my parents teach me (through their words and/or actions) about money, debt, religion, career success, dealing with authority figures, marriage, sex, parenting, trust, politics and other lifestyle issues? Are these beliefs my true beliefs or did I accept them without question?

- What beliefs are helping me in life, and what beliefs are holding me back?

You can come up with other questions. The point is, make sure you have truly made the transition from the "what does everybody else want" phase of life to the "what do I want to do with my time, talent and energy" phase.

Learning from others was a valid life phase. You needed to go through it. But, you don't need to stay in it forever. Jane and John would both appear to be incredibly high achievers on paper. However, they both crashed and burned for the same reason. They failed to challenge beliefs that were not serving them well. Don't wait until you crash and burn to challenge your beliefs and upgrade them if necessary. Maybe they are all OK…maybe they are not. *You* decide.

23
What's the Payoff?

What?

Whenever you encounter self-defeating behavior, you will almost always find some sort of associated psychological payoff driving the behavior. What do I mean by psychological payoff? It's the true underlying reason for the behavior. It's what a person hopes to get out of behaving in a certain way. And some of the payoffs will not necessarily seem logical. For example, as strange as it may seem, some people purposely do things to try and get others to yell at them or mistreat them. Maybe this is the only way they got much attention as a child. Perhaps they were repeatedly told as a child that they were "never going to amount to anything" and they are looking for evidence to support their "I'm not OK" life position. Who knows? Uncover the payoff and you are in a much better position to find a solution and eliminate or alter the self-defeating behavior.

So What?

Let's explore how a psychological payoff might drive an avoidance strategy. An avoidance strategy, which is a common form of self-defeating behavior, is an activity that may seem important, but is really just a cleverly disguised way of avoiding something *more important* that should be done. For example, let's dig deeper into the issue of why some people spend so much time on e-mails when they have more important things to do. All the e-mail tips in the world aren't going to help much if you don't understand and address the underlying psychological payoff for wasting time on e-mails. Once you understand this payoff, you can apply the same thinking to other avoidance strategies.

Here are a few of the more common psychological payoffs that drive avoidance strategies:

- *Avoidance* in itself is a psychological payoff. It allows people to avoid facing unpleasant feelings or situations. People use avoidance strategies to avoid legitimate fears (which are typically rational) or phobias (which are typically irrational). For example, people may have been given an assignment they believe is well beyond their capabilities. They may not even know how to get started on the assignment, *but they know how to check e-mails.* So checking e-mails becomes the path of least resistance. It is a path that offers some relief to their tension and stress. It makes them feel as if they are getting something done and helps them temporarily get the intimidating project off their mind.

- *Vindication,* or release from blame, guilt, suspicion or doubt, is a common psychological payoff. If people publicly rant and rave about how they can't get anything done because they are swamped with e-mails, they can come back later and use this as an excuse for not meeting project deadlines, or to explain the low quality of their work.

- *Validation* of a self-fulfilling prophecy, even a negative one, is important to some people. They may have been told they are worthless or feel worthless. I know it sounds weird, but some people go to great extremes to validate, reinforce and maintain their perceived life position. Checking e-mails when they have much more important things to do, accomplishes the exact results they desire...failure. Because failure, in turn, validates their belief that they are worthless.

Now What?

When you observe what appears to be self-defeating behavior, look for the psychological payoff. Eliminate the possibility of the payoff and you will stand a chance of eliminating or altering the behavior. In the three examples above you might:

- Offer additional training related to job responsibilities, or restructure the job to be more in line with current skill levels. These people are looking for relief from stress. That's the real issue driving their behavior. If you review Mihaly Csikzentmihalyi's (author of the book titled *Flow*) work on the psychology of optimal experience, you will discover there are four possible combinations in terms of job/worker challenges and skills. A job either provides low challenges or high challenges. And a worker either possesses low skills or high skills related to the challenges. In this situation, the worker's challenges exceed skills. Therefore, you must lower challenges, increase skills, or do some combination of the two.

- In the second case, unless this person's full time job is spending the day checking e-mails, you might consider calling his bluff. When you assign a project, make it clear that the e-mail excuse (or any similar excuse) will not be accepted as an explanation for lack of performance. You might also suggest restraint from publicly advertising the inability to handle job responsibilities. Rarely is this a good strategy for getting ahead in most organizations.

- If you recognize the third situation, you probably want to suggest the employee get professional help. The typical workplace is full of people with various forms of serious psychological baggage. It is a good idea to maintain a sense of appropriateness about when to turn a problem over to someone more equipped to handle it.

Remember, these are just a few examples of how payoffs can drive self-defeating behavior. My point is, improve your payoff recognition skills, and you will be in a better position to understand how you can help people improve their work performance. Start with these three payoffs: *avoidance, vindication* and *validation*. See if you can get better at recognizing them. See if you can come up with other versions of psychological payoffs that drive unproductive behavior. For example, what do you think are some of the payoffs for procrastination?

It is usually easier to determine other people's payoffs. But guess what? Psychological payoffs are also influencing your behavior. Go ahead and learn by observing others, but eventually get around to exploring some of your own counterproductive behaviors and the corresponding payoffs for the behaviors. When you understand them, you are in a much better position to deal with them. Don't avoid this problem. Think about it and do something about it!

24
What Do You Want to Be When You Grow Up?

What?

I have been surprised over the last 10 years by the number of people who have told me they are not sure what they want to be when they grow up. The surprising part is that most of these people are in their 40s, 50s, 60s and beyond. However, after thinking about this, it makes sense. I was one of these people about 10 years ago. As a result of my restlessness, I became a serious student of mid-life career changes and reinventing oneself...and then I reinvented myself.

If you are struggling with this issue, here are a couple of things I learned that might help. First, there are a lot of people thinking about this issue. You are not alone! And second, you've got to learn to get better at taking a position on certain issues if you want to implement a mid-life career transformation.

The process of career transformation does not mean you always have to quit your current job. This is certainly a possibility, but it is not the only way to get in alignment with your true calling in life. However, *getting in alignment with your unique life calling is a required step if you desire to live a joyful and productive life.* Unfortunately for many, this is a step very few people are willing to take.

So What?

So what is your position on taking a position? My first challenge is for you to take a position on one of the following beliefs:

- There is a specific purpose for my life, and knowing my specific purpose is an important aspect of a well-lived life.

- The issue of determining my true calling in life does not matter. It is not an important aspect of a well-lived life.

Do you agree with the first or second belief? Choose one or the other.

If you agree with the first belief, but *do not feel* you are currently in alignment with your life calling, this chapter will provide you with some clues on why you are in this position, and how to discover and get in alignment with your calling in life. If you prefer the second belief, I doubt if the rest of this chapter will be very meaningful to you. If you are unwilling to take a position on this issue, don't bother reading any further.

Here's my second challenge. If you believe we all have a specific life calling, it's time to ask yourself some additional questions. *Do you know your life calling? Are you in alignment with it?* Get stone-cold serious for a moment! Forget about any external considerations or influences. You're alone now, reading this book. No one else will know your answers and you don't have to tell anyone else until you are ready. *Are you really doing what you want to do with your life?*

In theory, I suspect most people would agree with the first belief, that we all have a life calling. According to one survey, 84 percent of the people questioned believe that every human has a unique purpose or destiny during their time on Earth. However, in the real world, do you think most people operate in alignment with this belief? Look around you. How many people do you personally know who seem to be in alignment with their true calling in life? How many people do you know who openly express the fact that they do not like their job?

Actually, there are some physiological reasons why so many people are not in alignment with their life calling. Unfortunately, most people make their initial career choice before they are 20 years old. At this point in life, the part of the brain that has the most to do with making good choices is not fully operational. This all has to do with how the brain evolves.

The human brain, as we know it today, evolved in three stages.

1. The first brain system to evolve took care of the basics of living: breathing, heartbeat, body temperature and other housekeeping-type functions.

2. Since humans cannot make it on their own early in life and need someone to care for them, the emotional brain evolved next. This second brain system has a lot to do with the formation of emotional bonds between parents and their offspring, and is the part of the brain that makes parents instinctively want to take care of their children. Without these emotional influences, creatures are known to literally "have their offspring over for dinner." Crocodiles have been known to casually eat their own eggs and then crawl off to look for something else to eat. Anyone who has raised a teenager knows there must be some biological force or something other than logic to get you to put up with some of the things you tolerate as a parent. Otherwise, we would end the

madness of parenting during the teen phase and crawl off to do something else.

3. The last brain system to evolve has to do with thinking, reasoning, judgment, making good choices, controlling impulses, organization, planning and such matters. It is sometimes called the thinking brain.

Two issues related to the way the brain evolved have the strong potential to send you down the wrong career path.

First, *your particular brain* evolved in much the same order and manner as *the overall human brain* evolved. So, most people make their initial career choice long before the thinking brain, which is critical to fully evaluating the implications of such a choice, is fully operational.

According to the results of brain scan studies, the thinking brain isn't fully online and ready to go until about the age of 23 for women and 25 for men. Prior to that, a young person's brain is pretty much in the "hold my beer and watch this" operational mode (or some equivalent if they don't drink beer). Daring, recklessness and poor judgment are often the order of the day. The recklessness can manifest itself in the form of physical daring, mental daring or both. This is also the period of time when people are much more susceptible to external influences, and there are usually plenty of people around to tell them what they should do with their life, which leads us to the second issue.

Second, the evolving brain develops in a manner similar to renovating a house. The garage might be converted to a den, a wall is knocked out here and there to expand a room, or maybe an extra bedroom is converted to an office. It's not the original design, but it serves your needs and you're comfortable with the way it is.

The original design for your brain was provided by nature. If all went well in the nine months prior to your first birthday (your real first birthday), the initial version of your brain was complete. And then nurturing forces took over and said, "Let the renovations begin!" Well-meaning parents, relatives, school teachers, coaches, professors, authors (including people like me), and others guided you along a predetermined path to adulthood. Your path was, for the most part, the path that *everyone else* thought was best for you. For example, your natural instincts might have guided you to pursue a career as an artist, painter, sculptor, musician or actor. But, the people who knew what was best for you may have decided to "renovate" the structures in your mind and help you develop different structures more supportive of being a businessperson, doctor, lawyer or engineer. And it's easy for the renovators to get their way since they control the life-sustaining resources at that point in your life. They are just like the contractors who renovate your house. It's not a good idea to screw around with them too much. They always seem to have ways of gaining the upper hand.

So most of us went through 16 to 20 years of renovation before getting to the make it or break it point where we finally had to take a position on what we were going to do, jettison the life support systems of our caretakers, and operate in a self-sustaining mode. In other words…get a job. This is all a formula for increasing the odds of defaulting to a comfort-zone position. What you may think was your choice when you were approaching your late teens or early 20s might not have really been your choice at all. The choice probably wasn't even made when you think it was. There is a strong likelihood that your career choice was actually made by other people at a much earlier time in your life. The renovated ideas of what you would be when you grew up were more comfortable to follow through on than your original ideas (if you can even remember your original ideas).

If you are a human being with a relatively normal brain, which developed in a relatively normal manner, there is an extremely good chance you may have missed your true calling in life. Some people figure it out sooner, some later…and some people never figure it out.

If you suspect you might need to consider some sort of career change or adjustments to be more in alignment with your calling, let's get practical and talk about some ways to do this.

Now What?

Here's my practical advice on how to identify your calling. *There is no practical way to identify your calling! Determining callings is not a practical matter! And nobody else can do it for you. That's the real issue.*

Once you figure out your calling, then you can get practical. Then you can call on your thinking, reasoning, planning brain and figure out some way – any way – to turn your life calling into a financially viable use of your time and energy. If you can't do that, then get ready to live a humble and meager financial life, and pursue your calling anyhow. You do not really have a choice if you desire to live a truly joyful and productive life.

As a matter of fact, if you are well into your career and you feel that you may have your ladder up against the wrong career wall, I'll almost bet you that your calling won't seem practical at all. It will most likely seem ridiculous to everyone, including you at first.

However, just so I don't totally abandon you and spend this entire chapter pointing out a problem and offering no solution, here is a "finding your calling" process you can try:

- Get finding your true calling on your mind. Set finding your calling *as your intention* and then direct a specific amount of your *attention* to your *intention*. Good targeting systems do two things, they lock on to the intended target and once locked on, they block out any distractions. That leads to the next suggestion.

- Reduce the busyness level in your life for at least 48 minutes a day so you will have time to think, reflect and feel as you explore various possibilities. This 48-minute suggestion has to do with the ramp-up time for mental processing and concentration. You can take longer each day if you'd like.

- Play the career version of the game *20 Questions*. Buy a package of index cards. They usually come 100 to a package. In this case, 20 questions may or may not be enough. You shouldn't need anywhere near 100 cards to figure this out, but if you do, buy another package. They're cheap!

- Each day during your 48 minutes, try your best to come up with at least one solid career and life-calling clue. Here are some possibilities:

    - Career status preference (owner, employee, partner, etc.)

    - Size of organization preference (small, medium, large)

    - Work preference (mental or physical)

    - Broad career category (Business or Arts and Sciences)

    - Work environment preference (indoors or outdoors)

- Work structure preference (structured or unstructured working hours)
- Geographical preference (northeast, southeast, northwest, southwest, mid-America)
- City size preference (small town, medium-sized town, city)
- National preference (domestic or foreign)

Come up with as many as you'd like, but *don't put the clue on an index card unless you feel very strongly about it.* For example, if you really don't care if you are an owner or an employee, don't create a card for that decision. Don't clutter up your cards with things that do not really matter to you. Use the shortest word or phrase you can think of to articulate the clue (one word is best).

- Don't shy away from considering any aspect of your career including working hours, geographic location, etc.
- Keep adding cards until you experience a genuine life-calling epiphany. Start with the easy choices, such as the examples listed above, and use the easy choices to generate ideas on some of the more complex choices. For example, after I made the Arts and Sciences choice, it prodded me to think of specific careers in these fields. So, I got out my encyclopedia and looked up Careers. At the end of the article there was a list of 139 career opportunities. I scanned the list and teaching, writing and psychology jumped out at me. So, I replaced my Arts and Sciences card with five new cards: teaching, writing, human behavior, joyful living, productivity (I replaced

and expanded on the psychology choice with additional cards that seemed to be more descriptive of what I really wanted to do). As you can see, there are only guidelines and not firm rules for this game. In the end, you get to play the game however you'd like.

How do you know when the game is over? That's it...*you'll just know!* You will feel it in your soul, so to speak. You will feel energized! After all, feelings are one of your best direct sources of knowledge. Everything else you "know" seems to come from external sources, like parents or teachers. When you get it right, all those parts of the brain I mentioned earlier will be in harmony about your decision. Your emotional brain will want to do it, your thinking brain will agree with the logic of your decision, and your housekeeping brain will respond quite well to it.

You will also know you're on the right path because the "hidden hands" of the universe will begin reinforcing and assisting you with your choice. Carl Jung called it synchronicity, some people call it coincidence. Call it whatever you prefer. Who knows, for the price of a package of index cards you might be able to figure out what you want to be when you grow up. Or you may be able to fine-tune your current choice and increase your ability to joyfully participate in life.

Discovering and pursuing your true calling in life is the ultimate strategy for living a joyful and productive life. I wish you much success in doing so.

What's Next?

As the old saying goes, "Sometimes it's a good idea to save the best for last." I saved the topic of discovering your true calling in life until last because I believe it is the most important topic in this book.

As a general rule, discovering and pursuing what you consider to be your true purpose in life is probably the most important step you can take if you desire to live a more joyful and productive life. Establishing priorities is significantly easier when you judge and measure your day-to-day actions in terms of how they help you successfully pursue your true life calling.

For those of you who agree that knowing your specific purpose is an important aspect of a well-lived life and are interested in further exploring this topic, visit www.dmetraining.com and download my paper titled, "How Your Life Calling Influences Your Productivity." It cost nothing to download the paper and I welcome your feedback on my comments.

Thanks to all of you who have attended *GO System* courses conducted by our network of certified trainers throughout the United States and Canada, those of you who have bought copies of my previous books and thanks to Dawson…wherever you are.

About the Author

Chris Crouch is the developer of the *GO System* training course. The course, widely taught in the United States and Canada by individuals, leaders, managers, professional organizers, coaches and corporate trainers, helps improve focus, organization and productivity in the workplace.

Chris has an impressive background in the financial services industry in sales, sales management and as an executive for a Fortune 500 company. However, his passion has always been reading and learning. Among other topics, he has spent years researching and studying both the mental and physical aspects of getting and staying productive – primarily for his own use. His goal was to find simple, easy-to-implement ideas that work in the real world. Others began requesting that he share this knowledge with them and their employees. Chris regularly writes, speaks and teaches on topics related to productivity. He is president and founder of DME Training and Consulting, and currently lives with his wife and youngest daughter in Memphis, Tenn.

Chris is always looking for ideas to improve productivity. If you have techniques that work for you and are willing to share them with him, or if you would like to discuss any of the ideas presented in this book, please write to Chris at cc@dmetraining.com.